168 HOURS

A STARTUP BUSINESS GUIDE
THAT RESPECTS YOUR TIME

CHRISTOPHER C. PAPIN

To my parents, Jerry and Carol Papin.

I grew up watching you build businesses not to escape life, but to build the life you wanted. Dad, I remember you everywhere in our community. People were always genuinely happy to see you and even today they continue to compliment the legacy you left behind. Mom, I watched and learned how you solve problems creatively. Co-locating your preschool with Dad's shop to minimize costs and maximize time with family. Leveraging your experience to launch a career transition into counseling that has impacted so many lives. You made business look like an art form, not a burden.

You taught me that the most important metric isn't profit. It's purpose! That flexibility matters. That family comes first. And that even when the unexpected happens (as it always does), a business built on solid footing and sound planning can endure and thrive.

To my brother Mike, who carries on Dad's legacy with excellence and integrity. Your resolve to succeed despite the circumstances is unmatched. You have amplified the lessons of our parents. Thank you for being with me shoulder to shoulder through it all.

And to the business owners I serve: I wrote this for you. For the moments when you question whether it's worth it. For the times you need permission to structure your business around your life. You have full permission not to sacrifice your life for your business. You can have both.

Copyright © 2025 Christopher C. Papin
Cover & Layout Design: Mel Wise

All rights reserved. No part of this book may be reproduced, distributed, or transmitted in any form or by any means, including photocopying, recording, scanning, or other electronic or mechanical methods, without the prior written permission of the copyright holder, except in the case of brief quotations embodied in critical reviews and certain other noncommercial uses permitted by copyright law.

Prohibition of AI Training:

This book and its contents, including but not limited to text, images, and design elements, are expressly prohibited from being used to train, develop, or improve any artificial intelligence (AI) systems, machine learning models, or similar technologies without the explicit written consent of the copyright holder. Unauthorized use for such purposes constitutes a violation of the author's intellectual property rights.

Uploading or distributing photos, scans, or any content from this book without prior permission is theft of the author's intellectual property. Please honor the author's work as you would your own.

Thank you in advance for respecting the author's rights.

168 Hours: A Startup Business Guide That Respects Your Time

Hardcover: 978-1-940498-50-8
Paperback: 978-1-940498-51-5
eBook: 978-1-940498-52-2

TABLE OF CONTENTS

AUTHOR'S NOTE 1

THE FORMAT 3

INTRODUCTION 5

PART I: THE BIG PICTURE

CHAPTER 1 9

CHAPTER 2 23

CHAPTER 3 29

CHAPTER 4 37

PART II: THE GAME PLAN

CHAPTER 5 63

CHAPTER 6 71

CHAPTER 7 77

CHAPTER 8 85

CHAPTER 9 93

CHAPTER 10 103

CHAPTER 11 109

CHAPTER 12 117

CHAPTER 13 125

CHAPTER 14 133

CHAPTER 15 141

CHAPTER 16 149

CHAPTER 17 159
CHAPTER 18 167
CHAPTER 19 177
CHAPTER 20 187

PART III: FUNDAMENTALS OF BUSINESS SUCCESS

CHAPTER 21 197
CHAPTER 22 205
CHAPTER 23 209

PART IV: BEHAVE LIKE A BUSINESS OWNER (BLABO)

CHAPTER 24 215
CHAPTER 25 223

PART V: THE EXIT

CHAPTER 26 229
CONCLUSION 237
YOUR JOURNEY, OUR EXPERTISE 239
ABOUT THE AUTHOR 241

AUTHOR'S NOTE

When I was a young athlete, I discovered something that would shape the rest of my life: I could see things developing before they happened. Not in a mystical sense, but through observation, positioning, and anticipation. On both the soccer field and playing football, I could read the play unfolding. I could anticipate where the ball was going, where my teammates needed to be, how to position myself for the best outcome. It wasn't magic. It was pattern recognition combined with preparation. Coaches would ask "how did you know to do that?" I would explain and they would compliment my actions.

Years later, I realized this skill translated far beyond sports. As a lawyer, CPA, and business advisor, I've spent all of my professional career helping thousands of entrepreneurs and businesses navigate their journeys. And I've noticed something consistent: the business owners who succeed aren't necessarily the smartest or the luckiest. They're the ones who *see* what's coming and *position themselves* accordingly.

I am grateful for the coaches, educators, and leaders around me who invested in developing this skill. They taught me to observe, to think strategically, and to understand that preparation meets opportunity and that's where luck lives.

Which brings me to why I wrote this book.

I've been fortunate enough to hold professional licenses. I've been trusted to guide businesses through their most critical decisions. And I've been blessed with insights that come from serving at every stage of the business lifecycle, from startup to exit. One of my law school professors, Bill Conger, said it best in his servant leadership speech: *if you've been given a gift, specifically gifts of a professional license or you carry the ability to lead, it is your duty to share it with the world and do something good with it.*

This isn't just a book about business plans or financial statements or legal structures. It's about positioning yourself — your time, your decisions, your focus — so that when opportunity shows up, you're ready. It's about understanding that the most successful athletes, leaders, and business professionals don't wait for luck to find them. They *manufacture* parts of that recipe. They prepare obsessively. They anticipate. They position.

You've been given 168 hours this week. So have I. So has every entrepreneur reading this. The difference between those who build thriving businesses and those who struggle isn't the number of hours — *it's what they do with them.*

Throughout this book, you'll find practical frameworks, real stories, and honest conversations about what business ownership actually requires. But more importantly, you'll find a philosophy: That business can be a vehicle for freedom, purpose, and the life you want to live. If you're willing to think like a coach, prepare like an athlete, and lead like someone who's been given a gift worth sharing, I've achieved the greater good Bill Conger challenged me to achieve... I will have shared a gift with the world and doing something with that gift.

My role is to help you see what's coming and show you how to position yourself for success. What you choose to do with that insight is entirely up to you.

The question isn't whether you'll get lucky. The question is: are you willing to do the work that makes luck possible?

Let's get to work.

THE FORMAT

This book is designed to help you establish your new business. It's organized into five parts, each building on the previous one to help you develop an actionable business plan based on your specific goals and ambitions.

PART I - THE BIG PICTURE

This part of the book explains theoretical concepts and illustrates several decisions you will want to consider when starting a business.

PART II - THE GAME PLAN

This part covers the key elements of a business plan. Part II begins with an executive summary featuring real-life examples that illustrate the various topics covered in subsequent chapters. Each chapter thereafter presents a core component of a business plan.

PART III - FUNDAMENTALS OF BUSINESS SUCCESS

Part III looks at the fundamentals that require the most attention to get your business started.

PART IV - BEHAVE LIKE A BUSINESS OWNER (BLABO)

Behaving like a business owner may seem simple, but it's often one of the most difficult elements of operating a business. Owners have a tendency to do "the fun parts" or "the parts they know" and neglect the rest. Part IV is designed to help you stay accountable for long-term success.

PART V - THE EXIT

All things have an end, and so, too, will your business. The final part aligns with the end of the business cycle and highlights what to consider while developing and operating your business to later facilitate "the end."

INTRODUCTION
YOU GET 168 HOURS

Every week, no matter who you are or what your goals may be, you're given the same resource as the most successful entrepreneurs, athletes, or leaders: 168 hours. Like a soccer team preparing for match day, how you structure those hours will determine whether you're building a winning business or watching opportunities slip through your fingers. How you train, who you pass the ball to, what plays you run — all impact whether you win or lose the game. If you're planning to start a business, you're not just starting a company. You're becoming a coach, a player, and a strategist for your own time. What you do with this time will matter more than it ever has. One of the most finite resources in business is time — and time is money, right?

Just like a soccer team doesn't spend all week on the field, you won't spend all 168 hours "doing business." But your off-the-field habits, like rest, learning, and planning, matter just as much as what happens during game time. Players need recovery, film study, and nutrition; entrepreneurs need rest, thinking time, and preparation. When you waste time without intention, it's like showing up to a match with no game plan, no conditioning, and no chemistry. The result? You're outpaced, outplayed, and exhausted.

Starting a business requires acknowledging where your time already goes and deciding if it supports your new role. You might need to make hard substitutions. If you're watching three hours of Netflix every night, that's like skipping practice. Your calendar reveals your priorities. If your dream is to launch a successful business, then your time needs to start reflecting that ambition.

Business owners are familiar with the quote, "Are you working *on* your business or are you working *in* your business?" A successful team has roles, systems, and structure. So should your week. Block out time to work *on* your business, not just *in* it. Some businesses you may be able to exclusively work "on;" however, most will be some combination of working "on" and working "in" the business. Create training sessions for planning and reviewing. Build a team of people who can support your journey. Every hour spent with intention is a pass completed, a goal attempted, a step closer to victory. The hours don't stretch, but they do stack, if you use them wisely.

You may not control how fast the clock moves, but you absolutely control what you do with the time you're given. Your 168 hours are exactly that: YOURS. What you use the time for is up to you. Use those hours well, and you'll start to see momentum, clarity, and traction. Misuse them, and you'll find yourself stuck in the midfield, chasing the ball while your goals drift further away. When the whistle blows, you don't get to ask for more time to catch up on things. The game is over. So, what are you doing with your time? Are you playing to win?

PART I:
THE BIG PICTURE

CHAPTER 1
GETTING SET UP FOR SUCCESS

Starting a business is a monumental decision that requires careful planning and introspection. Before diving into the practicalities, it's essential to understand the big picture. This chapter will help you understand what owning a business entails and how it aligns with your personal and professional goals.

From the earliest days I can remember, I was surrounded by the entrepreneurial spirit. Some of my first memories are of observing my mother and father, both business owners. My father, Jerry Papin, was an auto mechanic — but that label doesn't really do his talents justice. He was so much more than that to so many people. His talents included not only traditional auto mechanic skills but also skills that allowed him to play roles in racing, education, leadership, and mentorship.

I recall stories of his younger days, when he worked for another business in town refining his craft. Over time, he decided to leave the security of working for someone else to set out on his own. Carol Papin, my mother, was part of the driving force behind this decision and helped give him the confidence needed to set up his own shop.

My father was a charismatic person who found friends wherever he went. As a kid, I remember that he knew someone everywhere we went. Sometimes it was simply developing a relationship with an employee at a business we frequented, but most often it was someone in the community that he knew. As a child, I recognized that this was special because it did not happen to friends' parents.

I was in my single digits at the time, so I didn't really give this much thought. However, looking back, I think this may have been the first business lesson my father inadvertently taught me. What I took away from these interactions is that everyone was happy to see my father. He took a moment to engage in their lives, no matter where we went. Maya Angelou said, "People will forget what you said, people will forget what you did, but people will never forget how you made them feel." I think this sums up the lesson. My father was a likeable, positive person who made people feel engaged and welcomed. This is a major lesson for a business owner. How people feel about you, your business, and your team is important. Would your customers come up to you to say hello at the grocery store?

Why Owning a Business Could Be Your Ticket to the Life You Want

My parents' lessons were never designed to groom me to be in business; they were focused on making me a well-rounded, productive member of society. Nonetheless, I wonder if the spirit of entrepreneurship they espoused influenced me in some ways. My mom and dad were always parents first. They raised two boys, my brother Mike and myself. My brother and I both grew up to be business owners.

My mother, Carol, was also a business owner. Her formal education and work history was in early childhood education. She taught at local schools and found creative ways to engage youth. However, over time she sought greater flexibility in her life.

My first memories of my mother's business endeavors are deeply woven into my childhood because she opened a private preschool for kids. For those who don't remember, the 1980s and 1990s saw an increasing number of families with two working parents. This was a new development from the more traditional working father and stay-at-home mother. My mother's decision to start a preschool not only allowed her control of the business, education process, and curriculum, but also gave her an opportunity to teach me as I was at the appropriate age for this school. My brother is 12.5 years older than I am, so he was off to traditional primary and secondary education at this point.

My memories of this time are few because I was so young; however, I do clearly recall a few moments. In my mother's pragmatic fashion, her original school was located next to Dad's auto repair business. They shared two different spaces in the same building. I can remember my father taking me in, and my mother taking me home, which afforded both some flexibility. There were summers where I "went to work" with Dad but just played in the preschool space while he worked.

The lessons from this experience were lost on me until my twenties, when I watched friends start families and struggle with daycare schedules. These lessons were amplified when I started coaching middle school soccer during college, something I did to help earn money during school. One of my duties was to be present with players until parents picked up their kid after practice. I quickly realized that folks were struggling to juggle the demands of their busy schedules, because someone was always late.

About the same time, I started to appreciate the cost of rent. I was trying to find ways to have a decent place to live in college, which generally required living with roommates. I think Mom and Dad's original co-office locations were based on the same principles. It's a little easier if two businesses are sharing the rent. Mom found a way to minimize the transportation hurdle and save costs that also allowed her to spend more time closer to her family. My parents were able to spend time with my brother and I while also enjoying the flexibility of owning their own businesses and setting hours that accommodated their family structure at the time.

As I reflect on the early memories of the shared office location, I recognize the commitment Mom and Dad made to putting the family first. As my brother got into high school and college, he did some work for Dad's business. This put all four of us in the same place at the same time for a large part of the day. Although my time in preschool was short, there was still flexibility that spilled into other aspects of our lives. This allowed the freedom to make decisions differently than if Mom was teaching at a public school or Dad was working as an employee for a business. The business lesson here is that with ownership comes great flexibility — and this is only one of the many benefits it affords.

FREEDOM TO MAKE DECISIONS

One of the primary attractions of starting a business is the freedom it offers. In a traditional job, you have to follow directives from higher-ups, adhere to corporate policies, and sometimes compromise your ideas and values. As a business owner, you get to call the shots. This allows you to shape the business according to your vision and values, leading to a more satisfying and meaningful work experience. Not only do you have decision-making power, you also have full creative control. You can introduce new products, services, or processes that set your business apart from the competition as you wish. This freedom to experiment and implement new ideas can lead to significant breakthroughs and business growth.

SETTING YOUR OWN SCHEDULE

Being your own boss means you can set your schedule to fit your life, not the other way around. This flexibility is invaluable, especially if you have family commitments or other personal responsibilities. Unlike traditional jobs with fixed hours, owning a business allows you to work at times that suit you best. Whether you are a night owl or an early bird, you can structure your workday around your natural productivity peaks. This flexibility can lead to better work efficiency and a more enjoyable work experience. Flexibility also means you can manage your personal time more effectively. Need to take an afternoon off for a family event or a personal appointment? You have the freedom to do so. This ability to balance personal and professional commitments can lead to a more fulfilling life overall.

CONTROL OVER BUSINESS DIRECTION

When you own a business, you have the ultimate say in its direction. This means you can pivot strategies, explore new markets, or innovate without needing approval from others. This control can be incredibly empowering and satisfying, allowing you to pursue opportunities that excite you. You can set the long-term vision and goals for your business, ensuring they align with your personal values and ambitions. This strategic control allows you to build a business that reflects your ideals and aspirations, and to adapt quickly to respond to market trends, customer feedback, or competitive pressures. This agility can offer a significant competitive edge.

PASSION AND FULFILLMENT

Many people dream of turning their passion into their livelihood. Whether it's baking, crafting, consulting, or technology, starting a business allows you to immerse yourself in what you love. Passion is a powerful motivator that can drive you to overcome obstacles and persist through challenging times. When you are passionate about your work, it doesn't feel like a job and you are more likely to enjoy the journey and stay committed for the long haul. Passion also provides intrinsic motivation that keeps you going even when times are tough.

WORK SATISFACTION

When you are passionate about your business, work becomes more than just a means to an end. It becomes a source of joy and satisfaction, contributing to your overall happiness and well-being. Doing something you love day in and day out leads to a greater sense of fulfillment and personal satisfaction. It's not just about making money; it's about creating something that reflects your interests, values, and skills. A survey of Wharton graduates shows that those who became entrepreneurs tended to be happier than their peers, a testament to the work satisfaction that entrepreneurship can yield.[1]

FINANCIAL POTENTIAL

Starting your own business provides the opportunity to potentially earn more than you would in a traditional job. Your income is directly tied to the success of your business, and with hard work, smart strategies, and a bit of luck, you can achieve significant financial rewards. Unlike a salaried job where income growth is often limited by company policies or market rates, your business has the potential to scale and increase your earnings exponentially, a path to financial independence. Further, your business is an asset that can appreciate over time. Building a valuable business can significantly contribute to your net worth. This can provide you with the financial means to invest in other ventures, secure your retirement, or provide for your family. Additionally, a successful business can be sold for a significant profit, offering a substantial financial return on your years of hard work and investment.

FLEXIBILITY

I've already alluded to this with my parents' story: One of the greatest perks of running your own business is the flexibility it offers in terms of work hours and location. You are not confined to a 9-to-5 schedule or a specific workplace. Today, advances in technology make it possible to run many types of businesses remotely, allowing you to choose your work environment, whether it's a home office, a co-working space, or a beachside café. Such flexibility enables better integration of work and personal life. You can design a schedule that allows

---

[1] "Why MBA Entrepreneurs Are Happier Than Their Peers," *Knowledge@Wharton*, August 23, 2012, https://knowledge.wharton.upenn.edu/article/why-mba-entrepreneurs-are-happier-than-their-peers/.

you to pursue personal interests and spend time with loved ones without compromising your business commitments.

BALANCING PERSONAL COMMITMENTS

The flexibility of running your own business also means you can better balance personal commitments. Whether it's taking care of a family member, pursuing further education, or engaging in community activities, being your own boss allows you to integrate these aspects of your life more seamlessly. As a business owner, you can prioritize family time without the constraints of a traditional job. This ability to attend to personal matters while managing your business can lead to a more fulfilling and balanced life.

Practical Considerations: How to Prepare for the Realities of Business Ownership

Over time, my parents' businesses both grew. Ultimately, each needed more space, and Dad took over the entire location while Mom moved to a new location about four miles away, "on the way" between our home and Dad's business — an intentional choice. While these facilities were kept only for a short period of time, they were necessary to facilitate the next step for both businesses and our family.

At this point my brother was in college and helping in both businesses, primarily my father's. I was at an age where activities like soccer were starting to dominate my schedule. A five-minute trip from Mom's school to the soccer fields was a regular occurrence on weekends. All of our family's competing interests were within a reasonable drive of one another: my brother's college, our community church, my parents' businesses, my school and soccer practice field, and the shops we frequented. The strategic choice of business location allowed for maximum flexibility. However, just because there was flexibility does not mean there was no risk or stress.

Moving to a new location and going from paying half rent to two full rents was quite an undertaking. The new location also had to be set up and a new play area built, all while maintaining typical day-to-day activities. I can recall long days, nights, and weekends at Mom's new location to get the preschool up and running.

A few years later, the local public school system acquired the location Mom was leasing, so she had to consider what to do next. Ultimately, she chose to close the preschool and pursue continuing education. This allowed her to become a Licensed Professional Counselor (LPC) and transition into a new line of business in private counseling. She practices to this day.

Dad had transitions of his own to deal with, as his business success afforded him the option of transitioning to real estate ownership. At this point my brother was working in the business with my father. I can remember my parents looking at land and buildings, trying to figure out what the best next step would be. They chose to buy undeveloped land and build a new location for my father's business. Shortly after the building was finished, my mom obtained her LPC license, and they raced off to the next chapter of their lives.

In the years that followed, I finished middle and high school, becoming increasingly involved in soccer. With the family businesses set up, my parents had the flexibility to attend my games. My dad and my brother found ways to integrate themselves into the soccer support system by filming games, coaching, or being part of the booster programs. These opportunities benefitted both the family and the business, as the relationships developed from these activities ultimately ended up as customers of Dad's business.

Times were good…until they weren't. Unexpectedly, my father passed away from a heart attack at only fifty-seven years of age. Fortunately, my parents had the foresight to implement some estate planning to ensure the continuity of Dad's business and minimize any issues with his passing. My brother Mike was well-positioned to step in and keep it going. He continues to operate "Dad's auto business" more than two decades later — truly impressive when you consider that 70 percent of businesses do not make it to the next generation.[2] In both the next chapter and at the end of this book, you will be asked to keep the end of the business in mind — one of the many lessons learned from my family's entrepreneurship.

There are so many lessons that can be extracted from this segment of my parents' business journey. The story doesn't stop here, but this is a good opportunity to pause and reflect on some of those lessons. While the benefits of owning a business are numerous, it's important to recognize the practical considerations and challenges that come with it. Being aware of these factors can help you prepare mentally and practically for the entrepreneurial journey.

EXPECTING THE UNEXPECTED

The journey may not be linear and will likely have some unanticipated wrinkles. Developing a toolkit to navigate the business changes along the way is key. Change is inevitable. The cliché of finding comfort in your discomfort is a skill you need to develop as a business owner. As changes occur, you will be faced with choices. Sometimes these choices will feel like you are sacrificing because of the business. Other times these choices will feel like you are benefiting because of the business. Know that you will be faced with both types of choices and that you do not have control over when those choices will present themselves.

---

[2] George Stalk Jr. and Henry Foley, "Avoid the Traps That Can Destroy Family Businesses," *Harvard Business Review*, January-February 2012, https://hbr.org/2012/01/avoid-the-traps-that-can-destroy-family-businesses.

COMMITTING MONEY AND TIME, WITH NO GUARANTEES

Starting a business often requires a significant financial investment. This can include costs for equipment, inventory, marketing, and more. It's crucial to have a clear understanding of the financial requirements and to plan accordingly. Before jumping in, take time to build a **lean startup budget**. Identify what's essential vs. what can wait. Consider bootstrapping through pre-sales, service-based offerings, or leveraging platforms like Kickstarter to test demand before spending heavily. If you need capital, start small — microloans, community banks, or friends and family funding may be less risky than diving into large debt or giving up equity too early. Beyond the financial commitment, running a business also demands your time, especially in the initial stages. Many entrepreneurs find themselves working long hours to get their business off the ground. This can be challenging, particularly if you have other personal or professional obligations. Treat your time like capital. Map out your week. Where are your true time costs? Then prioritize high-leverage actions: sales over admin, customer validation over logo design. Delegate or delay tasks that don't move the needle. Even with limited time, consistency matters more than intensity. It's better to give 5 focused hours a week than to burn out in 50 hours.

Finally, this commitment of money and time comes with no guarantees. Entrepreneurship involves a degree of risk and uncertainty. There are no guarantees of success, and many businesses face challenges such as market competition, economic fluctuations, and changing customer preferences. It's important to be prepared for these uncertainties and to develop strategies for managing risk. For starters, you will have to accept that risk is part of the equation, but don't go in blind. Start by defining your *worst-case scenario. Wha*t happens if this doesn't work? Knowing that you can survive the downside helps you take smarter, more confident steps. From there, de-risk your idea as early as possible. Validate demand before you build. Talk to potential customers. Pilot your offer. The more you test, the more feedback you get and the less guesswork you're relying on. Build agility into your model. Keep your cost structure flexible. Track key indicators weekly. Revenue, lead flow, conversion, churn and other business health metrics matter. You can spot issues early and pivot quickly. Risk will never disappear, but good systems and honest metrics make it manageable.

MANAGING STRESS AND MAINTAINING BALANCE

Entrepreneurship can be stressful, and managing this stress is crucial for long-term success and personal well-being. Here are some strategies to help maintain balance and manage stress effectively:

- Delegation and support: Learning to delegate tasks and build a support network can help alleviate some of the burdens of running a business. Whether it's hiring employees, outsourcing tasks, or seeking advice from mentors, having support can make a significant difference.

- Self-care: Prioritizing self-care is essential. This includes taking time for physical exercise, maintaining a healthy diet, and ensuring you get enough rest. Mental health is equally important, and practices such as mindfulness, meditation, or talking to a therapist can be beneficial.

- Work-life boundaries: Establishing clear boundaries between work and personal life can help prevent burnout. Set specific work hours, create a dedicated workspace, and make time for hobbies and relaxation.

BUILDING A RESILIENT MINDSET

Resilience is a key trait for successful entrepreneurs. Building a resilient mindset can help you navigate the ups and downs of business ownership.

- Embrace failure as a learning opportunity: Instead of fearing failure, view it as a valuable learning experience. Each setback provides insights that can help you improve and grow your business.
- Stay adaptable: The business landscape is constantly changing, and adaptability is crucial. Be open to new ideas, be willing to pivot when necessary, and continuously seek opportunities for innovation.
- Cultivate a positive attitude: A positive attitude can help you stay motivated and focused. Surround yourself with positive influences, celebrate small victories, and maintain a hopeful outlook even in challenging times.

The Lessons This Book Holds for You

As you progress through this book, you will reap the benefits of the lessons I learned from my experience with my entrepreneurial family, as well as from my professional experience as a business advisor, attorney, and certified public accountant (CPA). I also serve on the Board of Directors for a local continuing care retirement facility. Throughout the book, I will share more professional experiences with you based on my career that will enable you to embark on your small business journey.

I have been a practicing attorney and CPA representing small business owners for the past seventeen years. I own and operate several businesses under one roof, including a law firm and CPA firm. I also take on public speaking and consulting work. In all phases of my business, I focus on supporting small business owners. Over the years, I have represented thousands of businesses at every possible stage, from startup to business closure. My focus is on service-based businesses that are privately held by one owner or a small group of owners and have less than one hundred employees. Typical revenues range from hundreds of thousands to several million in revenue.

In addition to my professional career, I think it's helpful to note that I've been a soccer coach for over twenty years and hold a United States Soccer Federation National D License. Although soccer may seem like it has nothing to do with business, the elements of sport heavily cross over into disciplines that can be successful for businesses. I stay engaged in coaching as a passion project. What is relevant to this book is that I am a staple in a developmental program that is the start to organized school soccer. My teams are at the seventh- and eighth-grade levels, which is when we start to introduce the fundamentals that are required to succeed at the high school, college, and professional levels.

The high school program, the next step for my players, is annually recognized as one of the best in the state, regularly winning the district championship and competing annually in the playoffs for the state title. Numerous players have played college soccer, and several have progressed to professional careers at various levels, including Major League Soccer. I have even had the privilege of coaching an MLS champion. I share this not to take credit for their hard work and skill, but to illustrate that our achievement is a collective effort built on a strong foundation, and I take great care in my role in helping form that foundation.

My role as a soccer coach is similar to that of a professional advisor. You could say I am both a soccer coach and business coach. Ultimately, *you* get the benefit of all these experiences. Hopefully, I have created an environment of truth in which you can see both the good and the bad through examples and stories. Obviously, I cannot build your business for you, but I can give you the tools and coaching needed to succeed. What you choose to do with them is up to you and will define your success.

CHAPTER 2
START WITH THE END IN MIND

Starting a business is a journey that begins with understanding your reasons for embarking on this path. Knowing your "why" is crucial because it serves as the foundation for all your decisions and actions. It's about having a clear vision of what you want to achieve and working backward to create a roadmap that leads you there. This chapter will guide you through identifying your end goals and aligning them with your reasons for starting a business.

According to the U.S. Bureau of Labor Statistics (BLS), about 20 percent of small businesses fail within the first year; 50 percent fail by the fifth year; and 65 percent fail by the tenth year.[3] Do not let these statistics deter you. Throughout my years representing clients, I have not experienced the same statistics as the BLS. I can count on one hand the number of actual failures that I have experienced within my client base.

Some of this is attributable to the fact that some of the work I do is transactional and non-recurring in nature. I would not know whether an LLC I created ten years ago is still in business if all they engaged us to do is form the LLC. However, the majority of the new businesses we create retain us for recurring work, using my CPA firm to help with tax and accounting needs. We must acknowledge that we have represented plenty of businesses that started for a purpose, operated until they achieved that

---

[3] Bureau of Labor Statistics, "1-year survival rates for new business establishments by year and location," March 4, 2024, https://www.bls.gov/opub/ted/2024/1-year-survival-rates-for-new-business-establishments-by-year-and-location.htm.

purpose, and then closed. This scenario is considered a "failure" to the BLS. In contrast, I consider failure a forced closing due to financial hardship or unsuccessful operation of the business.

I also think it is important to note that my client onboarding process seeks to work with engaged business owners. Please make no mistake in understanding here: Engaging a professional advisor is not going to guarantee business success. However, it is one of the indicators of successful businesses.

As you look forward to the end goal for your business, consider both the U.S. BLS statistics and my observations of those who succeed in our client base. Do you think you have all the information necessary to develop this thought process on your own? Likely the answer is no, but that's okay. A more realistic question is: are your thoughts developed enough to elaborate them to a professional who could then aid you in developing those plans into a more usable format? If not, this chapter can help you get there.

Common End Goals for Small Business Owners

Start with your vision for the future. Imagine where you want to be in five, ten, or even twenty years. What does your ideal future look like? This vision will serve as your guiding star, helping you navigate the challenges and opportunities along the way. Once you have a vision, you can break it down into specific, measurable, achievable, relevant, and time-bound (SMART) objectives. These objectives will help you stay focused and track your progress. However, you first need the vision. Ask yourself these questions to help shape it.

- Do you want to work until you die? For some, the idea of retiring is unappealing. They find fulfillment and purpose in their work and want to continue doing it as long as possible.

If this resonates with you, consider how your business can sustain your involvement over the long term.
- Do you want to sell your business? If so, to whom? When? For how much? Selling your business can be a significant end goal. Whether you plan to sell to a family member, an employee, or an external buyer, it's important to have a clear plan.
- Do you know how you will grow your business to this result? Growing your business to meet your end goals requires strategic planning and execution. Identify the strategies that will help you grow your business. This could include expanding your product or service offerings, entering new markets, or increasing your customer base.

Most small business owners (SBOs) start a business for a few primary reasons. I discussed these in the previous chapter: the freedom to make decisions and to set your own schedule, to have control over business direction, passion and fulfillment, work satisfaction, financial potential, flexibility, and the ability to balance personal commitments. Take a moment to consider which of those resonate with you.

Understanding your motivations and aligning them with your end goals is crucial for long-term success. Here's how the primary reasons for starting a business can support your end goals:

1. FINANCIAL POTENTIAL

Many business owners aim to generate sufficient income to support their current lifestyle. This involves planning for steady revenue streams and managing expenses effectively. Beyond supporting a current lifestyle, the financial success of your business can provide opportunities to fund future goals such as retirement, education, or other personal ambitions.

2. FLEXIBILITY, INDEPENDENCE, AND CONTROL

Flexibility allows you to balance your personal and professional life. This can lead to greater satisfaction and well-being. Independence and control enable you to create a business that aligns with your long-term vision. This sustainability is key to achieving your end goals.

3. LEVERAGING UNIQUE SKILLS, IDEAS, OR PRODUCTS

Many entrepreneurs are motivated by the desire to contribute to something greater than themselves. Whether it's solving a problem, serving a community, or making a positive impact, leveraging your unique skills or ideas can help you achieve this.

Pathways to Achieving Your Goals

Once you have identified your end goals and motivations, the next step is to determine how you will achieve them. There are various pathways to consider, each with its own advantages and challenges.

FULL-TIME EMPLOYMENT

Full-time employment provides a steady income, which can be beneficial for financial stability. Working full-time can also help you develop skills and gain experience that can be valuable when starting your own business.

PART-TIME EMPLOYMENT

Part-time employment offers more flexibility than full-time work, allowing you to dedicate time to your business while maintaining a source of income. This option can further help you balance work and personal commitments more effectively.

TEMPORARY EMPLOYMENT

Temporary employment provides short-term opportunities, which can be ideal if you need to focus on your business in the long run. Working in temporary roles can also give you a variety of experiences and help you build a diverse skill set.

CONTRACT ARRANGEMENTS

Contract work allows you to take on projects that align with your expertise and interests. You can choose the contracts you take, giving you more control over your work schedule.

GIG ARRANGEMENTS

Gig work offers diverse opportunities to earn income while pursuing your business goals. This option provides flexibility and can be a good way to supplement your income while building your business.

FREELANCE WORK

Freelancing offers independence and the ability to work on projects that interest you. You can leverage your skills and expertise to build a client base and generate income.

APPRENTICESHIP

Apprenticeships provide hands-on learning opportunities and mentorship, which can be valuable for skill development. Working closely with experienced professionals can give insight into the industry and help you build a network.

SELF-EMPLOYMENT

Self-employment offers the freedom to pursue your business ideas and create something of your own. Your efforts directly impact the success of your business, providing a sense of ownership and accomplishment.

Creating Your Roadmap: Making a Decision and Working a Plan

Once you have explored the various pathways, it's time to create a roadmap for achieving your end goals. This involves making informed decisions and working a plan that aligns with your vision and motivations. The next chapter looks at how to do just that.

CHAPTER 3
DO YOU LIKE YOUR PICTURE ENOUGH TO DO IT?

Having a clear picture of your end goals and motivations is crucial, but the next step is determining whether you are committed enough to pursue this vision. This chapter will guide you through evaluating your readiness and creating a roadmap that aligns with your goals. By expanding on the four key steps and completing a decision checklist, you'll be better equipped to decide if your picture is something you are ready and willing to bring to life.

Before establishing my various businesses, I was working at a firm that did much of the same work I do today. In fact, from time to time, I have the occasion to work with or refer work to my old firm. I have nothing but positive words to say about them. However, I recognized that the flexibility I wanted could not be achieved without making a change. Ultimately, I wanted some of the same benefits that my parents had through entrepreneurship. This was the leading factor for leaving and setting up my own firm.

Today, I can validate that this was the correct decision, but at the time, I was not able to articulate my vision and the steps I took to realize it as clearly as I can today. You can benefit from my own experience with the process and the years I've spent refining it by working with my clients to replicate it for them. It looks something like this:

Developing Your Roadmap

A big-picture overview of what achieving your vision will take can help you determine if you've got what it takes to pursue it. These steps can help you create that roadmap.

1. DEFINING YOUR PICTURE

The first step in creating a roadmap for your business is to define your picture clearly. This involves visualizing your end goals and understanding what success looks like for you. Spend time reflecting on what you truly want to achieve with your business. Is it financial independence, flexibility, or making a significant impact in your industry? Write down your vision in detail. Think about where you want to be in five, ten, or twenty years. How does your business fit into this long-term perspective?

Checklist for defining your picture:

- Have you clearly articulated your end goals?
- Does your vision align with your personal values and passions?
- Have you considered the long-term implications of your goals?
- Can you visualize what success looks like for you?

2. SETTING MILESTONES

Once you have a clear picture of your end goals, the next step is to break them down into smaller, manageable milestones. This makes the journey less overwhelming and helps you track your progress. Set SMART objectives that are Specific, Measurable, Achievable, Relevant, and Time-bound, and identify both short-term and long-term milestones. Short-term milestones help you build momentum, while long-term milestones keep you focused on the bigger picture. You can then determine which tasks are most critical to achieving your milestones and prioritize them accordingly.

Checklist for setting milestones:

- Have you set SMART objectives for your goals?
- Have you identified the immediate steps needed to start?
- Are your immediate steps aligned with your long-term vision?
- Do you have a mix of short-term and long-term milestones?
- Do you have a long-term plan in place for sustaining and growing your business?
- Have you prioritized your tasks effectively?
- Are your milestones realistic and achievable within your timeframe?

3. DEVELOPING A STRATEGY

Developing a strategy involves outlining the actions, resources, and timelines needed to achieve your milestones and end goals. Create a detailed action plan that specifies what needs to be done, by whom, and by when. This plan should include clear steps and responsibilities. It should also identify the resources you need, including financial, human, and technological resources. Ensure you have access to these resources or a plan to acquire them. Finally, there is the risk management angle: Consider potential risks and challenges that could arise and develop strategies to mitigate them.

Checklist for developing a strategy:

- Do you have a detailed action plan outlining necessary steps and responsibilities?
- Do you have the necessary support and resources to take these steps?
- Have you identified and allocated the required resources?

- Have you considered potential risks and developed mitigation strategies?
- Is your strategy flexible enough to adapt to unforeseen changes?

4. MONITORING AND ADJUSTING

The final step is to regularly monitor your progress and make necessary adjustments to stay on track towards your goals. Use tools and metrics to track your progress against your milestones and objectives. This could include financial reports, performance metrics, and regular reviews. Establish a feedback loop to gather insights from your team, customers, and other stakeholders.

Use this feedback to make informed adjustments to your strategy. Be open to adapting your plans as you grow and learn. Flexibility is key to navigating the entrepreneurial journey successfully.

Checklist for monitoring and adjusting:

- Do you have tools and metrics in place to track your progress?
- Do you have a process for reassessing your goals and strategies?
- Have you scheduled regular reviews to assess your progress?
- Have you established a feedback loop to gather insights and make improvements?
- Are you regularly reviewing and adjusting your strategy based on your progress and feedback?
- Are you open to adapting your plans as needed?
- Are you committed to continuous learning and improvement?
- Is your approach flexible enough to adapt to changes and new opportunities?

Resources to Help Develop Your Vision and Roadmap

Perhaps you need assistance in developing this thought process. There are lots of ways to get feedback, starting with talking to someone who knows you and asking their thoughts. Perhaps it is a spouse, best friend, colleague, or neighbor. Just start the conversation and listen to the feedback.

Another avenue is to research businesses online. With a quick search asking "what are successful businesses I can do from my house," I got multiple results, from home-based retail to creative digital businesses. There is no lack of ways to get information. The key is finding what is realistic and distilling all the information down to the information that is relevant to you.

Writing it all down may be helpful. I know I find it beneficial to see the list of features for a new software or service before purchasing it, for example. Break it down in a way that makes sense for you, whether that's a simple table, a chart, or a graph. You can use artificial intelligence (AI) tools to help.

Another way to get information is to interview someone (or multiple people) in the space that is of interest to you. If you want to do a personal training business, go find personal trainers and ask them for advice. Have a series of questions developed in advance and write down their responses. If the interviewee gets off track, help them get back on track by asking or re-asking a series of questions. Sometimes making the questions yes/no is helpful. You can always ask them to expound.

There are more formal ways that you can obtain information as well. There are training courses and online certifications you can get for free or for a nominal fee. There is no harm in using some time to see what is required and how to get there. With the right courses, you can gain a new skill, get certified, and be ready for business when you complete the training. Obviously, the more formal the training, the more time and money you will have to commit to it. Some licensing classes only require you to learn the material and pass the test. Frequently, the learning material isn't that expensive to buy.

Of course, you can seek advice from professionals. Whether you talk with a counselor, business coach, or professional advisor like an attorney or CPA, it is key that you go into those conversations with a clear objective in mind. All of these scenarios will likely cost you money and in some cases, this is a major investment. If you're a student, free options may be available at your school's career services office.

In all cases, if you get stuck, start asking questions of trusted people around you. They will steer you towards the objective you seek.

Making the Decision: Do You Like Your Picture Enough to Do It?

After defining your picture, setting milestones, developing a strategy, and planning for monitoring and adjustments, it's time to make a critical decision: Do you like your picture enough to commit to making it a reality? This is the moment to evaluate your commitment. Ask yourself:

- Do you feel passionate and driven to achieve your end goals? Your enthusiasm and motivation are key indicators of your commitment.
- Are you willing to invest the necessary time, effort, and resources to achieve your vision? Consider the sacrifices and commitments required.
- Do you have confidence in your roadmap and the steps you've outlined? Believe in your ability to execute the plan successfully.

I frequently use the phrase "talking about talking about it." Frequently, clients will say something like, "One day we should sit down and talk about my exit from the business. I don't think I'm ready for that yet, but I would be interested in knowing what my options are to help me consider what's next." Of course, this request is a very reasonable one. However, in my experience, most clients are more interested in talking about how one day we need to sit down and discuss <insert topic here>. When we ask them to schedule a time to do so, they say something like, "I'm not sure I have my thoughts together yet, so I'll let you know."

My team and I follow up on open items for clients. Either we meet and address the objective, or the client defers the meeting to another time, because they still don't feel ready to discuss the topic. So, again, we end up talking about talking about it and nothing more. This can happen for a number of psychological reasons, including avoidance and discomfort, lack of priority, poor communication skills, unaligned goals and interests, fear, and unconscious patterns.

The most successful clients set the meeting to talk about it and move the objective forward. The least successful ones continue "talking about talking about it." No matter the reason, committing to the next conversation is key. If you are serious about establishing a business of your own, no one is going to do it for you. You will have to take ownership of the next steps, even if you don't know what the next steps are. Our best clients say, "I don't know what to do next, but I want to keep this moving." This allows us to know their objective is to advance the cause.

Finally, I have to acknowledge one item in all of this that likely is a big driver for you and is for most businesses: Money! Money can be the singular reason things do not move forward. I realize that may be the case and it may sound harsh, but without proper financing, do not waste your time on all the other pieces of the puzzle. This is a key element to successful business and underfunding can cause business failures.

As a professional advisor, one of the most difficult items to reconcile with clients is whether the fees are worth the advice. When assessing the value of such expertise, I like to tell the story of the factory manager and the repairman:

A large factory had a critical piece of machinery that broke down, causing production to come to a halt. The factory's team tried everything they could to fix it but failed. Finally, they called in an expert with decades of experience in repairing such machines.

The expert arrived with a small toolbox, calmly inspected the machine, and listened to it carefully. After a few moments, he took out a small hammer, tapped a specific spot on the machine, and, like magic, it started running perfectly again.

The factory manager was overjoyed and asked for the invoice. The expert handed over a bill for $10,000.

The manager was shocked and demanded an itemized breakdown, saying, "All you did was tap it with a hammer!"

The expert provided an itemized invoice that detailed two items:

- Tapping with a hammer: $1
- Knowing where to tap: $9,999

This story illustrates two important lessons for you in your small business journey. First, you need a clear objective. The factory called an expert to achieve an objective because they couldn't figure it out on their own. The objective was clear: "Please fix the machine." It was not, "One day let's talk about how you might be able to help me fix the machine." Second, you will occasionally need to rely on the advice of others to achieve your objective. Does the value of your objective outweigh the value paid for the advice?

To bring this all together, it is important that you are clear in what you want to achieve and set a timeline to achieve it. With that in mind, you can find the right strategic partners to help you on your path.

CHAPTER 4
LEVERAGING EXPERTS IN THE FORM OF STRATEGIC PARTNERSHIPS

This chapter needs to start with the basics of strategic partnerships. First, what is a partnership? It's an arrangement between two or more parties to operate a business. The formality or informality at this point is not yet relevant. But remember, any attorney will make sure you put this agreement in writing to protect everyone involved. What is key for now is that two or more parties are coming together for a common purpose.

Next, it is important to define strategy. Simply put, a strategy is a framework used to achieve a goal. This concept is best illustrated by the efforts of a team coming together to win a game. Each team member has a similar objective, but ultimately each person has to execute their job within the bigger game plan to win. Within that framework, the team can achieve their goal of winning the game.

A strategic partnership is when multiple parties each fill a role to achieve a common objective. Strategic partnerships are different from formal partnerships, which may be contractual. A strategic partnership does not have to be. This is more of a collaboration between two or more parties who are aligning strengths. Perhaps there are various resources, expertise or common market access that allows both parties to achieve a result. The mutual benefit and intentional coordination can create a synergy that yields better results than if either side went about this on their own.

Although businesses may incorporate formal partnerships, it is far more common to see strategic partnerships. Visualize a business. Think about its primary objective. Then think about the various supporting activities that must take place to achieve the primary objective. Those supporting activities can be thought of as strategic partnerships. For example, UPS or FedEx are shipping companies. However, part of their success lies in their collaboration with the many retailers and manufacturers they serve. Neither UPS nor FedEx sells goods, but they have an overwhelming number of strategic partnerships that allow their core businesses to succeed. Similarly, you will need to develop strategic partnerships as a fundamental part of your business strategy to succeed.

I've already shared that I'm a former soccer player turned soccer coach. In any competitive sport, the objective is to win. How you choose to get to a win can take many forms and, over the course of a match, many factors can affect how and if that win is achieved. In reality, success on match day starts well in advance of the actual day of the competition. Let's take a minute to walk through a scenario that will be analogous to your need for strategy in business.

The Rainy Soccer Match: An Analogy for Adapting Tactics for Victory

The day started with a sense of anticipation. Both teams had been preparing for weeks for this crucial match which would determine the league champions. The Thunderbolts, known for their fast-paced, attacking style, were up against the Stonewallers, a team renowned for their solid defense and counter-attacks. As the teams warmed up on the pitch, the sky grew darker and soon heavy rain began to pour down.

The rain quickly turned the field into a slippery, muddy mess. Players struggled to maintain their footing and the ball skidded unpredictably across the waterlogged pitch. The Thunderbolts, who relied on precise passes and quick movements, found themselves at a disadvantage. Their usual strategy of intricate playmaking and swift attacks was ineffective in the treacherous conditions.

Recognizing the need for a change, Coach Rivera called the Thunderbolts to the sideline during a break in play. His voice barely rose above the sound of the rain, but his message was clear.

"Listen up, everyone! This weather isn't going to change, so we need to adapt our game. Forget the fancy footwork and quick passes. Here's what we're going to do ..." He laid out a revised strategy, calling for more direct play, greater physicality, simplified passing, and defensive solidarity.

As the game resumed, the Thunderbolts implemented their new strategy. The midfielders and defenders started launching long balls towards the flanks, where their speedy wingers could chase them down. The forwards adjusted their runs, anticipating the ball's unpredictable movements. The simplified passing in the defensive third minimized mistakes and kept the Stonewallers from capitalizing on turnovers.

By the time the final whistle blew, the Thunderbolts could celebrate a hard-won victory. The rain-soaked field had tested their resolve, but their ability to adapt had made the difference. Coach Rivera's tactical adjustments had turned a challenging situation into a winning strategy.

The rainy match against the Stonewallers became a defining moment for the Thunderbolts. It taught them the importance of flexibility and adaptability in the face of adverse conditions. By recognizing the limitations imposed by the weather and adjusting their tactics accordingly, they had turned the elements to their advantage. It was a lesson in resilience and strategic thinking that would serve them well in future challenges, both on and off the pitch.

If you have not yet started to see the analogy, I want to make this a little more direct. Drawing on analogies from athletics can be really powerful to help others relate and see your business vision. Soccer is very unique to other sports because of its constant fluidity. It is ever-changing, adapting, and unpredictable. These are some of the reasons it's referred to as "The Beautiful Game." In business, the landscape is the same: There are ever-changing conditions despite a common goal. Perhaps the conditions are favorable to your objectives. Perhaps they are unfavorable to your objectives. A strategy will provide parameters for your success, keeping you focused on your final goal while being flexible enough to adapt as needed to get there.

So, what's in a strategy? A lot! There are both defined and undefined elements. What is most important is to try to recognize that a strategy will stretch beyond the defined or spoken pieces into intangible, hard-to-define concepts. Your effort to create clarity around your strategy will be ongoing and ever-changing. If you can recognize that these concepts are constantly evolving like the game of soccer, you are on the right path to helping define your future success.

The Role of Strategic Partners in Your Business Success

In the world of business, success is rarely achieved in isolation. Surrounding yourself with the right strategic partners can significantly enhance your chances of success. These partners bring diverse expertise, perspectives, and resources that can help you navigate challenges, seize opportunities, and achieve your business goals. This section explores the critical role of strategic partners such as CPAs, lawyers, bankers, and others, and how leveraging their expertise can propel your business forward.

For small business owners, strategic partnerships can provide the expertise and support needed to address complex issues and make informed decisions. Here's why strategic partnerships are essential:

- Access to expertise: Strategic partners offer specialized knowledge and skills that may be outside your core competencies. This access to expertise can help you solve problems more efficiently and effectively.
- Resource sharing: Partners can provide resources such as funding, technology, and networks that you may not have access to independently.
- Enhanced credibility: Associating with reputable partners can enhance your business' credibility and reputation, making it easier to attract customers, investors, and other stakeholders.
- Risk mitigation: Partners can help identify and mitigate risks, protecting your business from potential pitfalls.
- Innovation and growth: Collaborative efforts often lead to innovative solutions and strategies that drive growth and competitive advantage.

Different types of strategic partners bring different types of expertise to the table. Here's a quick overview of some common strategic partners for small businesses and what they offer.

CERTIFIED PUBLIC ACCOUNTANTS (CPAS)

CPAs are financial experts who can provide invaluable insights into managing your business's financial health. Their services include:

- Financial management: CPAs can help you set up robust accounting systems, manage cash flow, and prepare financial statements.

- Tax planning and compliance: CPAs ensure your business complies with tax regulations, helping you avoid penalties and optimize tax strategies.
- Budgeting and forecasting: CPAs assist in creating budgets and financial forecasts that guide your business decisions and long-term planning.
- Business advice: Beyond numbers, CPAs offer strategic advice that can improve your business operations and profitability. They can analyze financial performance and provide strategic planning.
- Investment advice: CPAs can also offer advice on investment opportunities and capital allocation to maximize returns.

LAWYERS

Lawyers play a crucial role in ensuring your business operates within the legal framework. Their expertise includes:

- Business formation: Lawyers can advise on the best legal structure for your business, whether it's an LLC, corporation, partnership, or sole proprietorship.
- Contracts and agreements: Lawyers draft, review, and negotiate contracts to protect your interests.
- Intellectual property: Lawyers help secure patents, trademarks, and copyrights to safeguard your intellectual property.
- Risk management: Lawyers help you manage risks by ensuring your business adheres to all relevant laws and regulations (compliance). They also handle legal disputes and litigation to minimize business disruptions.
- Employment law: Lawyers advise on employment law to avoid issues related to hiring and firing employees, as well as workplace policies.

BANKERS

Bankers provide essential financial services that support your business operations, including:

- Loans and credit lines: Bankers offer various financing options to meet your business needs, from startup capital to expansion funds.
- Cash management: Bankers help manage cash flow with services like treasury management and payment processing.
- Investment advice: Bankers provide guidance on investment products and strategies to grow your wealth.
- Facilitate connections: Bankers introduce you to potential investors, partners, and clients through their networks.
- Financial planning: Bankers assist in developing financial plans that align with your business objectives.
- Advisory services: Bankers can offer advice on mergers, acquisitions, and other strategic decisions.

BUSINESS CONSULTANTS

Business consultants bring specialized knowledge to address specific challenges in areas such as:

- Marketing: Consultants can develop marketing strategies to build your brand and attract customers.
- Operations: Consultants streamline operations to improve efficiency and reduce costs.
- Technology: Consultants can implement technology solutions that enhance productivity and competitiveness.

MENTORS AND COACHES

Mentors and coaches provide guidance, support, and motivation to help you stay focused on your goals. They can:

- Share experience: Mentors offer insights based on their own business experiences.
- Provide accountability: Mentors keep you accountable for your goals and actions.
- Offer encouragement: Mentors support you through challenges and celebrate your successes.

Integrating Expertise for Success

These partners provide the support, resources, and insights needed to overcome challenges, seize opportunities, and achieve your vision. Each professional brings a unique perspective, contributing to a well-rounded approach that covers all critical areas of your business. This holistic support ensures that every aspect of your business, from finance and legal to marketing and operations, is addressed. This allows you to make well-informed decisions based on comprehensive advice and insights. In this way, your business is positioned for long-term success with a solid foundation and strategic plan.

Remember, the power of collaboration lies in the collective strength and diverse expertise that each partner brings to the table. Embrace these partnerships, foster strong relationships, and work together to turn your business dreams into reality. A collaborative approach involves actively engaging with your strategic partners to leverage their expertise and insights. Here's how to foster effective collaboration:

- Maintain open and transparent communication with your partners to ensure everyone is aligned and informed.
- Clearly outline each partner's role and responsibilities to avoid confusion and overlap.
- Schedule regular meetings to discuss progress, address issues, and explore new opportunities.

- Foster a culture of mutual respect where each partner's contributions are valued and appreciated.

Building a successful business is a complex and challenging endeavor, but you don't have to do it alone. By leveraging the expertise of strategic partners such as CPAs, lawyers, bankers, business consultants, and mentors, you can navigate the complexities of business ownership with confidence.

I own and operate both a CPA practice and a law practice. Over the course of my career, I have had the pleasure of serving thousands of business owners in varying degrees of representation. I help business owners clarify objectives, set milestones, create financial plans and budgets, develop funding strategies, and craft growth strategies. From advising startups on the best legal structure for their business to ensuring they are adhering to relevant laws and regulations, I provide support at multiple levels.

My comprehensive expertise as a CPA and attorney, combined with strategic partnerships with other professionals, positions my clients for success. By leveraging this support, they can confidently navigate the challenges of business ownership and achieve their vision. That is the power of strategic partnership.

A Glimpse Behind the Scenes: Results from the Field

Professionalism requires that I meet certain standards at all times and accordingly, I must maintain confidentiality. Of course, I am a lawyer so the joke would be that I need to use as many confusing words as possible to describe what comes next. (Smile... that was a joke!!!) Although I do want to be as accurate as possible, I do need to incorporate a disclaimer to protect certain information. Its jargony but necessary.

Disclaimer: The examples presented in this document are inspired by real-life situations and experiences in my professional practice. However, to respect the confidentiality and privacy of my clients, names, identifying details, and certain situational specifics have been adapted or fictionalized. While the core challenges, strategies, and solutions reflect genuine scenarios and insights, any resemblance to actual persons, entities, or events is coincidental and unintentional. These adaptations ensure that client confidentiality remains protected while allowing readers to gain valuable lessons and perspectives from these examples.

This book is intended for informational purposes only and does not constitute legal, tax, or other specific professional advice. All representations are general in nature and may not apply to every situation. Readers are strongly encouraged to consult with qualified professionals such as attorneys, CPAs, or financial advisors to confirm the accuracy and applicability of the information to their unique circumstances.

The tools and strategies outlined throughout this book are the same fundamental principles applied in each of the scenarios presented. These foundational approaches have been instrumental in solving complex business challenges across a variety of industries. These proven methods serve as a roadmap for readers to navigate their own entrepreneurial journeys effectively.

Medical Office Example: Building a Healthy Practice

Dr. Emily Collins had a vision that extended beyond her stethoscope. A well-regarded physician with over a decade of experience in hospital settings, she yearned for a practice of her own. One that offered not only exceptional medical care but also an environment where patients felt genuinely cared for and staff felt inspired. It wasn't just about medicine; it was about creating a space for trust, healing, and professional collaboration.

This dream brought Dr. Collins to my office. She was brimming with ideas yet burdened by the complexities of translating her vision into reality. Financing had been secured and she had identified a high-traffic location in a growing suburb. But like many new business owners, she was overwhelmed by the intricate layers of establishing and operating a business. Her concerns were as diverse as they were urgent: choosing the right entity structure, recruiting a cohesive team, managing her practice's finances, and ensuring long-term sustainability.

As we began unpacking her needs, the enormity of the task became clear. Dr. Collins wasn't just building a practice. She was building a business that had to balance the clinical, operational, and financial elements seamlessly.

ENTITY STRUCTURE PLANNING: THE BACKBONE OF THE BUSINESS

The first major hurdle was deciding how to structure her business. A sole proprietorship would have been the simplest route, but it came with significant liability risks. An LLC offered liability protection but didn't maximize the tax benefits she needed. After analyzing her income projections, growth ambitions, and liability concerns, we ultimately decided on forming an S-Corporation.

This structure provided:

- Liability protection. Shielding her personal assets from potential lawsuits, a critical consideration in the litigious healthcare industry.
- Tax efficiency. Allowing her to draw a reasonable salary while taking distributions that weren't subject to self-employment tax.
- Growth flexibility. Enabling her to bring in additional investors or partners down the line if she chose to expand.

We also formalized a comprehensive operating agreement that outlined governance rules, financial protocols, and an exit strategy. This agreement ensured the practice was equipped to scale or transition smoothly in the future.

PERSONNEL AND DEVELOPMENT: BUILDING A TEAM, BUILDING A CULTURE

As a physician, Dr. Collins understood the importance of a reliable team but underestimated how difficult recruiting and retaining talent can be. We crafted a step-by-step hiring plan to find the right blend of skills and personalities that aligned with her patient-centered philosophy.

Dr. Collins needed to fill several roles: nurses, a receptionist, a medical assistant, and a practice manager. I advised her to:

- Partner with a local healthcare staffing agency to streamline the initial screening process.
- Incorporate personality assessments into interviews to gauge alignment with her practice's culture.
- Offer competitive salaries coupled with non-monetary incentives such as flexible schedules and professional development opportunities.

The result was a team that brought both clinical expertise and a shared passion for personalized patient care.

Recruiting a team was only the beginning. Retention proved to be a bigger challenge, especially in a market where experienced medical staff were in high demand. Within the first year, Dr. Collins faced unexpected turnover when two nurses left for higher-paying hospital positions.

In response, we implemented a robust retention strategy:

- Professional growth: Annual stipends were introduced for continuing education, allowing staff to enhance their skills and certifications.
- Wellness initiatives: Monthly wellness workshops covering topics from stress management to yoga underscored Dr. Collins's commitment to her staff's well-being.
- Recognition programs: A quarterly recognition system celebrated team contributions, from stellar patient feedback to innovative solutions for workflow improvements.

These changes transformed the practice into a workplace of choice, reducing turnover and increasing employee satisfaction scores.

CASH FLOW ANALYSIS AND MANAGEMENT: NAVIGATING EARLY STRUGGLES

One of the most significant challenges was managing cash flow during the early months. Medical practices often face delayed reimbursements from insurance companies, and Dr. Collins's was no exception. Combined with high upfront costs — equipment leases, salaries, and a five-year commercial lease — the practice teetered on the brink of financial instability within its first three months.

We approached cash flow management systematically:

- Line of credit: Dr. Collins established a $100,000 line of credit, providing a safety net for payroll and other critical expenses during reimbursement delays.

- Patient payment policies: The office began requiring partial upfront payments for procedures likely to experience delayed insurance reimbursements, helping stabilize income.
- Expense prioritization: Non-essential purchases, such as aesthetic office upgrades, were deferred until the practice reached consistent profitability.

Additionally, I worked closely with Dr. Collins to develop a monthly cash flow forecast. This tool gave her clarity on projected inflows and outflows, allowing her to anticipate and address potential shortfalls proactively.

STRATEGIC GROWTH: LAYING THE GROUNDWORK FOR EXPANSION

By the end of the first year, the practice had stabilized and was earning a positive cash flow. Dr. Collins's reputation for personalized care began attracting patients through word-of-mouth referrals. However, maintaining growth required strategic adjustments.

We conducted a market analysis and identified an opportunity to expand services into wellness offerings, including physical therapy and nutritional counseling. This diversification not only tapped into existing patient needs but also aligned with Dr. Collins's vision of holistic care.

Key steps included:

- Hiring specialists. Dr. Collins brought on a part-time physical therapist and a certified nutritionist, expanding the scope of services without overextending her budget.
- Starting marketing campaigns. Targeted digital ads highlighted the practice's new offerings, leading to a 15 percent increase in appointments within three months.
- Optimizing workflow. The addition of new services necessitated adjustments to scheduling and staff

responsibilities. A workflow consultant was hired to streamline operations and ensure efficiency.

THRIVING IN A COMPETITIVE MARKET

Two years later, Dr. Collins's practice stands as a model of success. The patient roster has doubled, and the practice boasts a 98 percent satisfaction rate. The office's expanded services have become a key differentiator, and her team operates like a well-oiled machine.

Key outcomes include:

- Financial stability. The practice is now fully self-sufficient, with strong cash reserves and a declining reliance on credit.
- Team excellence. Employee retention has risen to over 90 percent, thanks to the supportive culture Dr. Collins has cultivated.
- Strategic positioning. The addition of wellness services has cemented the practice as a one-stop destination for patient health, giving it a competitive edge in the region.

Reflecting on her journey, Dr. Collins often expresses gratitude for the structured guidance she received. By tackling key pain points — entity structure, personnel management, and cash flow planning — her vision of a thriving, patient-focused practice became a reality. Today, she not only delivers exceptional care but also leads a business that stands as a testament to the power of preparation, adaptability, and perseverance.

Professional Scenario: Guiding Growth for a Licensed Architect

Jonathan Miller was a licensed architect with a thriving solo practice. Known for his innovative designs and attention to detail, he had earned a strong reputation in his region. Despite his success, Jonathan felt he had hit a plateau. His client base was steady, but his business growth had stagnated. He was managing every aspect of his practice himself, from designing projects to handling client contracts and overseeing billing. The workload was overwhelming, and he recognized that he needed a strategic plan to scale his business sustainably.

Jonathan came to me with several pressing concerns:

- How to position his business for growth without sacrificing the quality and personalization his clients valued.
- How to adapt to changing market conditions, including increasing demand for environmentally sustainable architecture.
- How to optimize his revenue streams and reduce inefficiencies in his current processes.

His passion for architecture was evident, but he was struggling to translate that passion into a scalable business model.

STRATEGIC GROWTH AND MARKET ADJUSTMENTS

Jonathan's first major challenge was finding a way to grow his practice while staying true to his core values of client-focused design. Together, we crafted a strategic growth plan that prioritized sustainable expansion.

I advised Jonathan to position himself as a leader in sustainable design, a growing niche in his industry. This involved:

- Updating his branding to highlight his expertise in green architecture.
- Developing marketing materials that showcased his environmentally conscious projects.
- Expanding services. To diversify his revenue streams, Jonathan introduced consulting services for developers seeking guidance on sustainable building practices. This

allowed him to leverage his expertise without the time-intensive commitment of full project management.
- Partnership development. We identified opportunities to collaborate with real estate developers and construction firms, creating partnerships that generated a steady pipeline of projects. These partnerships allowed Jonathan to focus on design while outsourcing administrative and construction oversight.

CASH FLOW ANALYSIS AND REVENUE OPTIMIZATION

While Jonathan's business was profitable, his revenue was inconsistent, largely due to the long payment cycles typical in architecture. He often found himself waiting months for final payments after project completion.

To address this, we implemented a comprehensive cash flow management strategy:

- Revised payment structure: Jonathan introduced a phased payment system, requiring clients to pay in installments aligned with project milestones. This ensured steady cash inflows throughout the project lifecycle.
- Retainer agreements: For consulting services, we implemented retainer agreements, providing Jonathan with a predictable monthly income stream.
- Expense management: By analyzing his operating costs, we identified areas where he could reduce expenses, such as switching to cost-effective design software without compromising quality.

These changes stabilized his cash flow, giving him the financial confidence to invest in growth.

PERSONNEL AND DEVELOPMENT

As Jonathan's client base grew, so did his workload. It became clear that he couldn't handle every aspect of the business on his own. We developed a staffing plan to build a small, efficient team:

- Hiring support staff: Jonathan hired a part-time administrative assistant to manage contracts, invoices, and client communications, freeing him to focus on design.
- Junior architect: Bringing on a junior architect allowed Jonathan to delegate routine tasks such as drafting and preliminary design work. This not only reduced his workload but also improved project turnaround times.
- Mentorship and training: To ensure quality, Jonathan invested time in mentoring his new hires. This created a cohesive team that upheld his high standards.

With the right team in place, Jonathan's practice became more scalable, enabling him to take on larger and more complex projects.

ADAPTING TO MARKET CHANGES

The architecture industry was rapidly evolving, with clients increasingly demanding sustainable, energy-efficient designs. Jonathan embraced this trend, but doing so required investing in new tools and staying ahead of industry developments.

Jonathan pursued additional certifications in green building standards, such as LEED (Leadership in Energy and Environmental Design). This not only enhanced his expertise but also made his services more marketable.

We also evaluated and implemented cutting-edge design software that streamlined workflows and supported sustainable architecture. While the upfront investment was significant, the long-term efficiency gains justified the cost.

Finally, we focused on client education. Jonathan began offering workshops and webinars to educate potential clients on the benefits of sustainable design. This positioned him as a thought leader and generated new leads.

BUILDING A SUSTAINABLE FUTURE

Two years later, Jonathan's practice is thriving. His reputation as a leader in sustainable architecture has opened doors to larger, more lucrative projects, and his diversified revenue streams have made his business more resilient. Key outcomes include:

- Revenue growth. By diversifying his services and optimizing cash flow, Jonathan increased his annual revenue by 40 percent.
- Team development. His small but dedicated team has enabled him to take on more projects without compromising quality or client satisfaction.
- Market leadership. Jonathan's expertise in sustainable design has set him apart from competitors, securing his position as a go-to architect for environmentally conscious projects.

Reflecting on his journey, Jonathan expressed pride in how far his practice had come. By addressing key pain points — strategic growth, cash flow, and personnel development — he built a business that not only aligns with his values but also positions him for long-term success.

Real Estate Owner Scenario: Managing Growth in a Residential Portfolio

Rebecca Turner was an ambitious real estate investor who had built a portfolio of five single-family rental homes over the course of eight years. Her properties were located in a growing metropolitan area, and she had enjoyed a steady stream of tenants and income. However, as her portfolio grew, so did the complexities of managing it. Rebecca began to feel overwhelmed by the administrative burdens, tax implications, and strategic decisions required to maintain and expand her investments.

Rebecca approached me seeking clarity on several pressing issues:

- Whether her existing business structure protected her assets and optimized her tax situation.
- How to effectively manage cash flow to cover expenses like property maintenance, taxes, and occasional vacancies.
- Whether she should consider expanding her portfolio by acquiring more properties or diversifying into other types of real estate.

While Rebecca was passionate about real estate, she recognized that her current approach lacked the structure and foresight necessary to sustain long-term success.

ENTITY STRUCTURE PLANNING: PROTECTING ASSETS AND REDUCING RISK

One of Rebecca's primary concerns was protecting her personal assets from liability. Up to this point, she had owned her properties individually, which exposed her to significant risks. If a tenant filed a lawsuit or an accident occurred on one of her properties, her personal savings and assets could be at stake.

We reviewed her situation and determined that forming a series of limited liability companies (LLCs) was the best solution. This structure provided:

- Liability protection. Each LLC owned one or two properties, isolating risks and limiting exposure in the event of a legal dispute.
- Tax advantages. As a real estate investor, Rebecca could take advantage of pass-through taxation, allowing her to deduct expenses such as depreciation, maintenance, and interest.
- Scalability. The LLC structure made it easier for Rebecca to partner with other investors or transfer ownership in the future.

To streamline management, we also set up a holding company that owned the individual LLCs, simplifying her accounting and reporting requirements.

CASH FLOW ANALYSIS AND MANAGEMENT: WEATHERING FINANCIAL PEAKS AND VALLEYS

Rebecca had experienced inconsistent cash flow due to tenant turnover, unexpected repairs, and varying rental income. To address this, we developed a comprehensive cash flow management plan:

- Emergency reserves: Rebecca established a reserve fund equal to six months of property expenses. This cushion allowed her to cover costs during vacancies or unexpected repairs without dipping into personal savings.
- Rental pricing strategy: A market analysis revealed that Rebecca was underpricing two of her properties. By adjusting rents to align with market rates, she increased her monthly cash flow by 15 percent.

- Streamlined expenses: We negotiated better rates with service providers, such as landscapers and HVAC technicians, saving her thousands annually.

Additionally, I worked with Rebecca to create a detailed cash flow projection for each property. This allowed her to anticipate shortfalls and allocate resources more effectively.

STRATEGIC GROWTH AND MARKET ADJUSTMENTS: EXPANDING THE PORTFOLIO

With her existing properties stabilized, Rebecca was eager to expand her portfolio. However, she was uncertain about the best approach: Should she acquire more single-family homes, or diversify into multi-family units or commercial properties?

To guide her decision, we conducted a thorough market analysis:

- Local trends: The analysis revealed strong demand for affordable housing in her area, making multi-family units an attractive option.
- Financing options: By leveraging the equity in her current properties, Rebecca secured favorable financing for a small duplex. This allowed her to diversify her portfolio without overextending financially.
- Risk assessment: Multi-family units offered reduced risk compared to single-family homes, as a vacancy in one unit wouldn't result in zero rental income.

We also explored potential partnerships with other investors, enabling Rebecca to access larger opportunities while sharing the financial burden and risk.

PROPERTY MANAGEMENT AND EFFICIENCY

Managing multiple properties had become a time-consuming task, leaving Rebecca little time to focus on strategic growth.

We implemented systems to streamline operations and reduce her workload:

- Property management software: Rebecca adopted a digital platform to track rental payments, maintenance requests, and lease renewals. This reduced administrative overhead and improved tenant satisfaction.
- Outsourcing: Rebecca hired a property management company to handle tenant interactions, freeing her to focus on portfolio strategy and new investments.
- Maintenance plans: We created a proactive maintenance schedule to address issues before they escalated into costly repairs, saving Rebecca time and money.

BUILDING A RESILIENT REAL ESTATE BUSINESS

Two years later, Rebecca's real estate portfolio has grown to include eight properties, including the duplex she acquired as part of her expansion plan. By addressing her pain points head on, Rebecca transformed her investment hobby into a structured and sustainable business. Key outcomes include:

- Asset protection. The LLC structure has shielded Rebecca's personal assets while providing a framework for growth.
- Financial stability. With improved cash flow management and diversified revenue streams, Rebecca has built a resilient business capable of weathering market fluctuations.
- Operational efficiency. By leveraging technology and outsourcing, Rebecca has reduced her workload, giving her the freedom to focus on long-term goals.

Looking back, Rebecca attributes her success to the strategic planning and foundational tools she implemented early on. With her business thriving, she is now exploring opportunities to mentor other aspiring real estate investors, passing on the lessons she learned along the way.

PART II: THE GAME PLAN

CHAPTER 5
THE EXECUTIVE SUMMARY

I am confident you have heard some version of the adage regarding seeing all the trees in the forest versus looking through the forest tree by tree. In short, it is a tale of two perspectives.

In the heart of the vast Eldenwood Forest, two young saplings grew side by side, Alder and Birch. Though they shared the same soil, drank from the same rain, and swayed in the same wind, they saw the world in very different ways.

Alder, eager and ambitious, always spoke of all the trees: how the forest as a whole stretched for miles, how it provided shelter for creatures big and small, how its collective strength withstood storms. "We are part of something grand," he would say. "Each of us contributes to the mighty Eldenwood."

Birch, on the other hand, believed in seeing things tree by tree. He took time to notice the unique patterns of bark on their trunks, the way each tree's roots twisted differently into the earth, and how no two leaves were exactly alike. "The beauty of the forest," Birch would counter, "is in the details, in each individual tree's story."

One day, a great fire raged through Eldenwood. Smoke curled through the air, and flames licked at the forest floor. The trees whispered in fear.

Alder, seeing the fire from above, called out, "We must act to protect the entire forest! If we don't find a way to stop it, Eldenwood will be lost!" He urged the tallest trees to spread their branches wide, shading the younger ones from the heat. He encouraged the animals to carry seeds deeper into the safe parts of the woods, ensuring that Eldenwood would live on, no matter the damage.

Birch, watching the fire at ground level, moved in a different way. He called out to individual trees, guiding them to bend where the fire was weakest. He noticed where the soil was still damp and urged the roots to pull up the last bits of moisture to slow the burn. He directed the birds to carry water from the nearby stream, tree by tree, helping each one endure the flames.

When the fire finally died out, Eldenwood remained standing. Alder and Birch, side by side once again, realized something important that day. To truly thrive, the forest needed both the big picture and the small details. The strategy of caring for the forest and the strategy of caring tree by tree. Both perspectives are needed.

Eldenwood endured, stronger than ever, with Alder and Birch standing tall, side by side, forever growing and forever learning from each other.

Similarly, as a business owner, you're going to need to balance the big picture and the small details. A comprehensive business plan can do just that, starting with the executive summary. The Cambridge Dictionary defines the executive summary as "a short text that gives the most important facts or ideas contained in a longer document."[4] The executive summary balances the big picture and the small details of a business plan, combining them into a big-picture document that summarizes each small detail.

Because this process can be intimidating, my advice to you is to just start. It does not matter where you start or how well. Just start. You will have more than enough opportunities to refine

---

[4] Cambridge Dictionary, s.v. "Executive Summary," accessed June 20, 2025, https://dictionary.cambridge.org/dictionary/english/executive-summary.

your thinking. My experience working with clients tells me to give a little push here, so again: Just start! The key is to get started and let the process build from there. Some may stagnate and need to restart, but more frequently things do not progress because clients never start.

At our very first practice of any soccer season, my role as head coach is to assess and ask questions. In that first practice, I am not expecting every player to show technical perfection. Above all, I am looking for effort. Why does this matter to you? Because if you do not put in the effort, you will not get the results. This is training day one. No one cares if your draft executive summary is good or bad. All that matters is that you are present and working on it. Writing and business skill sets are developed over time through practice and dedication. Now is your chance, so get out your notes and get started.

The Executive Summary: The First Impression

The executive summary is the most critical part of your business plan. If you have been an athlete, consider the warm up period when you watch the other team. Were they organized? Did someone just "look the part?" Maybe the opposite is true? Another way to think of it is the kickoff to a soccer match. The first few minutes that sets the tone for the game. The executive summary provides a snapshot of your business, capturing the essence of your plan in a few pages. The key components of an executive summary include the following:

MISSION STATEMENT

Purpose: The mission statement briefly describes your business's purpose and values, much like a team's commitment to fair play, sportsmanship, and excellence.

Example: "Our mission is to deliver innovative health solutions that improve the quality of life for our customers, just as a soccer team strives to bring joy and excitement to its fans."

According to The Walt Disney Company website: "*The Mission of the Walt Disney Company is to entertain, inform, and inspire people around the globe through the power of unparalleled storytelling, reflecting the iconic brands, creative minds, and innovative technologies that make ours the world's premier entertainment company.*"

BUSINESS CONCEPT

Summary: A concise summary of your business model and what makes your business unique, akin to outlining the team's unique style of play and strategy.

Example: "We offer a subscription-based service that provides personalized fitness plans, similar to how a soccer team might develop customized training programs for each player."

Disney Example: The business model is built around storytelling, brands and technology.

GOALS AND OBJECTIVES

Short-Term and Long-Term Goals: Outline your business's immediate goals and future aspirations, comparable to a team's seasonal objectives and long-term vision for championships.

Example: In the next year, we aim to expand our customer base by 20 percent and develop partnerships with leading fitness influencers, much like a team targets winning local tournaments before aiming for national titles.

Disney Example: Environmental goals include having a positive impact on communities by creating content that inspires connection with the planet and working with industry partners to create a healthier world for future generations.

Before we continue with the remaining elements, I want to expand on the three Walt Disney Company examples above. My goal is not to do a case study on a company, but merely to illustrate an important point using a familiar company. Whether or not you see the Walt Disney Company in the same manner that I do is wholly irrelevant to whether or not the mission statement hits the mark or not. In everyone I speak to about this, there is a recognition that Walt Disney Company does exactly what their mission statement enumerates: "to entertain, inform, and inspire." The important takeaway is to recognize that your actions must be consistent with what is written. Walt Disney Company hits the mark; the business concept, goals, and objectives are consistently on message with consumer expectations for the company. The same should be true for your business.

PRODUCTS OR SERVICES

Overview: A brief outline of what you offer, similar to a soccer team's core strategies and tactics.

Example: "Our core product is a mobile app that delivers personalized fitness plans and nutritional advice, akin to a team's playbook that guides them through each match."

MARKET OPPORTUNITIES

Summary of Market Analysis: Highlight the market needs and opportunities your business aims to address, much like identifying weak points in opponents' defenses.

Example: "There is a growing demand for personalized health solutions in the market, and we are poised to fill this gap with our innovative app, similar to how a team exploits an opponent's defensive weaknesses."

COMPETITIVE ADVANTAGE

Unique Selling Proposition: Explain what sets your business apart from the competition, similar to a team's unique style of play or standout players.

Example: "Our app uses advanced AI to create highly personalized fitness plans, offering a level of customization that our competitors cannot match, just like a star player's unique skills can make a team unbeatable."

FINANCIAL HIGHLIGHTS

Key Financial Projections: Provide a snapshot of your financial projections and funding requirements, much like outlining the team's budget and funding needs for the season.

Example: "We project a revenue growth of 25 percent annually for the next five years, with a funding requirement of $1 million to expand our development team, similar to a team's need for investment to secure top talent and improve facilities."

Crafting a Compelling Executive Summary — Best Practices

The executive summary is your business plan's first impression. It should be concise, engaging, and tailored to your audience. By clearly summarizing your mission, business concept, goals, products or services, market opportunities, competitive advantage, and financial highlights, you set the stage for a compelling and convincing business plan. Just as a strong start can lead a team to victory, a well-crafted executive summary can pave the way for your business's success.

Follow these best practices to get it right:

- Be concise and clear: Your executive summary should be brief and to the point, just as a coach's halftime speech needs to be concise to motivate the team quickly. Aim for no more than two pages, focusing on the most critical aspects of your business plan.
- Engage your audience: Use compelling language to capture the reader's attention, much like a team's opening play

aims to captivate the audience. Highlight your business's potential and why it is an exciting investment opportunity.
- Focus on key information: Include only the most vital information that provides a clear picture of your business, similar to how a coach's strategy focuses on key plays. Avoid jargon and overly technical details that can detract from the main points.
- Tailor to your audience: Customize your executive summary to the needs and interests of your potential investors or stakeholders, much like tailoring a team's strategy to exploit an opponent's weaknesses. Understand what your audience values and emphasize those aspects of your business.

Launching a successful business is akin to coaching a championship team. Since this is about your business, you are the head coach, and this book is your playbook. It's designed to guide you through each scenario that needs to be considered for success. The executive summary is the start to your business plan: your game plan. A solid foundation and a well-thought-out structure are imperative to ensure longevity and resilience in business. Your business plan, which we discuss in the next chapter, provides that foundation.

CHAPTER 6
THE GAME PLAN IS YOUR BUSINESS PLAN

A business plan is the cornerstone of any successful business. Think of it as your game plan. Without it, you're like a team stepping onto the pitch without knowing the strategy. Your business plan details your plays, strategies, and goals. It's your roadmap through the season, helping you navigate the competitive landscape and attract the right sponsors and supporters.

This document details your business model, goals, and strategies. It outlines your target market, competitive analysis, marketing strategy, and financial projections. A well-crafted business plan not only guides your operations but also attracts investors and partners. It provides a clear vision and direction, helping you stay focused and aligned with your objectives.

Having a vision in your head is one thing, but getting that information out of your head and into a sketch of your entrepreneurial endeavor is another. This is our goal.

Three Questions to Ask When Formulating a Business Plan

Many components of the business plan are covered in the chapters that follow. Before we get too deep into the details, I want you to take a step back and ask yourself three questions.

1. IS THIS BUSINESS PLAN FOR ME OR FOR AN EXTERNAL STAKEHOLDER LIKE A BANK, INVESTOR, OR BUSINESS PARTNER?

If your business plan is for yourself, you need enough detail to explain it to a middle schooler. If it is for a third-party stakeholder, you need a level of detail that meets or exceeds their expectations, which is likely more detailed than one solely for yourself. Consider creating versions that achieve both goals.

2. IS MY BUSINESS WELL KNOWN AND WIDELY UNDERSTOOD?

If the model is widely understood, you can utilize examples and market references to help educate the readers. If the model is not, you will have to expand on your thoughts and visions to make sure others can see and understand it like you do. Consider asking friends to give you feedback along the way.

3. HOW WILL I USE THIS BUSINESS PLAN IN NINE DAYS, ONE YEAR, THREE YEARS, TEN YEARS?

Focus on the long-term vision first. If you do not see a use beyond one year, this is likely more operational in nature and should be addressed elsewhere. Details are important, but this document is not designed to explain "how the sausage is made." Unless, of course, you have a unique and new way to do exactly that! The point: Operational details go in the operations manuals. Often, entrepreneurs get lost by focusing on the wrong things when working on the bigger picture.

The Purpose and Importance of a Business Plan

A business plan serves multiple purposes. Primarily, it acts as a strategic guide for your business operations. By clearly defining your business model, goals, and strategies, you establish a framework for making decisions and solving problems. It also serves as a communication tool to attract investors, partners, and key stakeholders. A well-prepared business plan demonstrates your commitment, understanding of the market, and ability to execute your vision, just as a detailed playbook shows a coach's preparedness and strategic thinking.

A business plan includes several key components, each serving a specific function:

- Executive summary: A concise overview of your business, summarizing the key points of your plan, similar to the opening strategy a coach uses to kick off the season.
- Business description: An outline of your business, its mission, and its unique value proposition, akin to defining the team's identity and playing style.
- Market analysis: A detailed analysis of your industry, target market, and competition, much like scouting reports on other teams and understanding the league.
- Organization and management: A description of your business's organizational structure and the management team, akin to detailing the coaching staff and team roster.
- Products or services: An explanation of the products or services you offer, similar to the various tactics and formations the team employs.
- Marketing and sales strategy: A plan for how you will attract and retain customers, much like the outreach to fans and sponsors.

- Funding request: If seeking funding, an outline of your funding requirements and future financial plans, akin to securing sponsorship deals and funding for the season.
- Financial projections: Detailed financial forecasts, including income statements, cash flow statements, and balance sheets, similar to the team's budget and financial planning.
- Appendices: Any additional information, such as résumés, permits, or lease agreements, akin to additional training materials and resources for the team.

Your Roadmap to Success

A robust business plan is essential for the success of your business. It serves as your game plan, providing a clear vision and direction for your business. By detailing your business model, goals, and strategies, you establish a framework for decision making and problem solving.

In working with my client base, I have found that multiple different examples of the same concept can help illustrate the idea to my audience. Communication can be tricky. You can give an example, tell the story that goes with it, ask if it is understood, and have your audience acknowledge that it is understood — but you can still miss the mark. This may be the case in a few scenarios as we evolve through this book together; however, all the various experiences, stories, and suggestions are based on real life and anchored in truth.

I think a quote from Socrates might supplement my point above: "The wise man learns from everything and everyone, the ordinary man learns from his experience, and the fool knows everything better." If you blend your own experience with observations and external learning, your business journey can be much more robust.

The Socratic method is a teaching tool where you educate others through a series of questions to help develop the students' beliefs, skills, or understandings. With my legal training, it is hard to separate this process from who I am. Law school is rooted in this philosophy, and the Socratic method of teaching is still used in law school today.

In the Part II chapters that follow, I conclude by asking you a few leading questions to help you develop a business plan. This will be supplemented by an example — a sample business plan for a fitness professional wanting to get into podcasting — which will allow you to further develop your own plan on your own while learning from the example in front of you. Admittedly, this sample plan will not be beautifully polished, but rather a raw form of a business plan that might mirror yours in its early stages. Hopefully, this will give you at least one other experience to utilize and reflect upon to make your own plan even better.

CHAPTER 7
MARKET RESEARCH IS THE SCOUTING REPORT

Imagine you're about to enter a high-stakes game without any knowledge of the other team. You don't know their strengths, weaknesses, or strategies. Success, in this case, would rely entirely on luck — and that's not a sustainable strategy. The same applies to business. You can't operate effectively without understanding your market, competitors, and customers. Market research is your scouting report. It's the foundation that helps you analyze, predict, and strategize for success.

Before the game, scouts study the opposing team's tactics, identify key players, and examine past performance to predict how they might play in the upcoming match. Similarly, market research gives you a comprehensive understanding of the environment in which your business operates. By studying market trends, competitors, and customer behaviors, you can develop strategies to outmaneuver the competition and make informed decisions that position your business for long-term success.

When you're in the big leagues, you have the resources to study other teams' films, send scouts to opponents' games, break down the statistics and turn them into analytics, and utilize this information to create a competitive advantage. Not all have those resources available to them. However, that doesn't mean that you completely skip this step. You need to have a pulse on your market, no matter how formal or informal of a process.

Why Market Research Matters

Market research answers critical questions about your business environment. It reveals opportunities and helps you avoid costly mistakes by showing you where your business fits in the marketplace. A well-researched market plan allows you to:

- Identify your target market. Just as knowing your opponent's lineup is essential, understanding your target market is crucial. Who are your customers? What are their needs, preferences, and behaviors? Market research helps you paint a detailed picture of your audience so that you can tailor your offerings and marketing strategies accordingly.

- Analyze the competition. In sports, it's essential to know not just your game plan but also the strengths and weaknesses of the other team. Competitor analysis is the business equivalent. By studying what your competitors are doing well — and where they are falling short — you can carve out your unique competitive advantage.

- Spot trends and opportunities. Much like a scout notices emerging talents and new plays, market research helps you stay ahead of industry trends and identify growth opportunities. Whether it's adopting a new technology or meeting a rising consumer demand, staying ahead of the curve ensures that your business remains competitive.

Gathering the Data: Your Playbook for Success

There are two main types of market research: primary and secondary. Each plays a vital role in creating a complete scouting report for your business.

PRIMARY RESEARCH: FIELDWORK ON THE FRONTLINES

Primary research involves collecting new data directly from your potential or existing customers. Think of this as the firsthand observations a coach makes by attending games in person. You're getting insights straight from the source. Methods of primary research include:

- Surveys and questionnaires. Engage with your target audience by asking them about their preferences, buying habits, and pain points. Surveys help you identify the exact needs of your customers and whether your business is addressing them.
- Interviews and focus groups. Talking directly to customers provides deeper insights into how they feel about your product or service. Much like one-on-one discussions with players can reveal critical insights into team dynamics, customer interviews can uncover invaluable feedback.
- Product testing. Sometimes, the best way to understand what the market wants is to put your product directly in front of consumers. Testing different iterations of your product allows you to see what resonates with your audience and refine your offering based on real-world feedback.

SECONDARY RESEARCH: LEARNING FROM THE PAST

Secondary research involves analyzing data that already exists. Just as scouts review tapes of past games, you can use reports, studies, and statistics to gather insights into market trends and consumer behavior. Sources of secondary research include:

- Industry reports. These are published by research firms and provide in-depth insights into market size, growth, and key players. Using these reports can give you a broader view of the industry and help benchmark your business.
- Competitor analyses. By going over your competitors' marketing strategies, products, and customer reviews, you can identify gaps in the market and areas for improvement within your business. Are they scoring goals where you aren't? Are there opportunities they're missing?
- Online databases and publications. Government publications, trade associations, and online databases often provide valuable market data. Utilize these resources to stay informed about the external forces shaping your industry.

Interpreting the Results: Turning Data into Strategy

Data by itself won't win the game — you need to interpret it and use it to inform your business strategies. Much like a coach adapts their game plan based on the scout's report, you must adjust your business strategy based on what your market research reveals.

One way to do this is with a SWOT (Strengths, Weaknesses, Opportunities, Threats) analysis. This is a tool that helps you organize your findings. Knowing your strengths and weaknesses is like knowing your team's best players and weak spots. Identifying opportunities and threats helps you stay agile and prepared for external forces that might affect your business.

Scouting for Success

Market research is the backbone of your business strategy. Once you've gathered data on who your customers are and what they want, you can refine your marketing and product development strategies to better meet their needs. Just as a team refines their playbook after reviewing game tapes, you should continuously revisit your customer profiles and adapt your strategies.

Just as a successful coach never stops scouting the competition, you should never stop researching your market. This will help you stay ahead of industry trends, maintain customer satisfaction, and identify new opportunities for growth. This is a continual process. In the same way that scouting is ongoing throughout the season, market research is not a one-time task. Markets shift, consumer preferences evolve, and new competitors emerge. By regularly conducting market research, you ensure that your business remains competitive and adaptable.

In business, just like in sports, knowledge is power. The more you know about the field you're playing on, the better prepared you are to win. Even if you do not have the resources to have a full market analysis, make sure you find a way to gather some limited feedback so that you understand factors relevant to you. Sometimes it is as simple as asking your customers how you can improve.

So, lace up your boots, grab your scouting report, and get ready to play to win. Your market research will be the guide that helps you navigate the competitive landscape and come out on top.

Questions for You to Answer, Plus a Podcast Example to Consider

Market research will help you refine your business idea. As you think about your business idea, ask yourself the following questions:

- What is the problem I am trying to solve?
- Is the problem permanent or is it temporary?
- Will I be able to solve this problem on a recurring basis?
- How will people be able to find out that I can solve this problem?

As we transition to the podcasting analogy, let's answer the questions above from the perspective of a service provider, a fitness coach:

What's the problem?

People want support in living a healthy or healthier lifestyle.

Is this permanent or temporary?

Both. There is likely a use case for a permanent lifestyle change and a long-term relationship that can develop. Perhaps there will be life-long customers; however, reality and statistics likely prove that the customers you will have will be temporary and/or cyclical.

Will I be able to solve this problem on a recurring basis?

Absolutely. Regular sessions and recurring sessions are a norm in this industry. However, there is a likelihood that some clients learn what to do and do it on their own or do not stay committed.

How will people find out I can help?

There are a number of ways, but frequently the easiest is to start by working at a gym as a trainer. You can tell your network of friends and utilize word of mouth or social media. You can also do some form of targeted advertising.

Why would a fitness trainer want to start a podcast?

You might think of three paths to success. The first would be as an advertising piece or a way to share your knowledge in a bulk format. Perhaps the podcast is a free lead to a paid service. The second option could be to appear as a guest expert on someone else's podcast. This keeps costs down and reaches a larger audience. The third would be to turn the podcast into a social media money maker. There are lots of ways to monetize content and if your information is popular enough, maybe you do not even need clients.

A SAMPLE SWOT ANALYSIS

Continuing with our example of the fitness coach who wants to get into podcasting, I was able to quickly create this SWOT analysis using only online research:

Strengths

This would give the trainer a duplicatable platform to share her knowledge and wisdom about the industry. Perhaps the trainer's personality will shine through and connect with people in a way that compels them to take action. If this is your passion, you will not only make it a lifestyle, but you will regularly be in the industry and relevant with industry trends.

Weakness

The costs and other competing voices in the same space might cause the trainer to get lost in the noise of all the people doing a similar thing. Large fitness companies might have a monetary advertising advantage and utilize personalities/celebrities to gain attention.

Opportunity

Health and fitness is a $22.4 billion industry.[5] Capturing even a small market share is a very realistic possibility. For example, a trainer targeting six sessions per day at $100 per session could make $114,000 per year (six per day, five days a week, forty-eight weeks a year).

Threats

Competitive "bigs" in the industry like gyms, at-home videos, DIY workout equipment, and pharmaceutical companies seem like insurmountable competitors. Connecting with a client base without a facility may be a deterrent.

---

5   Health & Fitness Association Staff, "The U.S. Health and Fitness Industry Is a $22.4 Billion Economic Powerhouse," Health & Fitness Association, May 7, 2024, https://www.healthandfitness.org/about/media-center/press-releases/the-health-and-fitness-industry-is-22-4-billion-economic-powerhouse-3/.

CHAPTER 8
FUNDING AND FINANCIAL MANAGEMENT

Imagine a team trying to win a championship without the right equipment, training facilities, or travel budget. Success would be nearly impossible. In business, your "resources" come in the form of capital — money that allows you to launch, sustain, and grow. Just like a sports team needs funding for uniforms, coaches, and travel, your business needs funding for day-to-day operations, expansion, and unexpected challenges. Proper financial management is the playbook that helps you navigate these financial waters, ensuring that you have enough resources to stay competitive throughout the entire game.

In this chapter, we'll explore how securing funding and managing your finances with precision is essential to the health and success of your business. This isn't just about having money in the bank — it's about having a strategy for how to allocate and manage those funds effectively. Much like setting a budget for a sports season, you need to plan how your business will operate within its financial constraints while still reaching its goals.

Sources of Funding: Building Your War Chest

Just as a team needs sponsors and ticket sales to fund their operations, your business needs capital to fund its operations. There are several sources of funding to consider, each with its own advantages and disadvantages.

1. Personal savings: Many entrepreneurs use their personal savings to fund the initial stages of their business. While this shows a strong personal commitment to the business, it also carries personal risk.
2. Loans: Traditional bank loans or Small Business Administration (SBA) loans can provide the funding necessary for startup or expansion. However, loans require repayment, usually with interest, and approval can be a lengthy process.
3. Investors: Seeking funding from investors (venture capitalists, angel investors, or even friends and family) is another option. Investors often provide not only capital but also mentorship and access to their networks. However, they will likely want equity or control in your business.
4. Grants and competitions: Some businesses may qualify for grants or win competitions that provide funding without requiring repayment. While extremely beneficial, such funds are not always easy to obtain.
5. Crowdfunding: Platforms like Kickstarter or GoFundMe have become popular avenues for entrepreneurs to raise funds. Crowdfunding allows you to test the market's interest in your product while also raising capital.

Budgeting: Your Financial Playbook

Once you've secured the necessary funding, the next step is budgeting — allocating your financial resources in the most effective way. Budgeting ensures that you have enough cash to cover expenses while still investing in growth opportunities. Here is what a budget should cover.

OPERATING EXPENSES

These are the costs associated with running your business day-to-day, such as rent, utilities, payroll, and supplies. Without planning for these, you risk running out of cash when you need it most.

CAPITAL EXPENDITURES

These are the funds spent on major purchases like machinery, office space, or technology. Just as a sports team might invest in a new stadium or training center, your business might need to invest in equipment or facilities that will enable growth. These expenses should be planned carefully, as they require a significant upfront investment.

CONTINGENCY FUND

Every business needs a contingency fund — a cushion for unexpected expenses or downturns in revenue. In sports, you always need backup players in case of injury. Similarly, a financial contingency plan ensures that your business can weather unexpected challenges like market fluctuations, equipment failure, or slow periods.

Financial Management: The Key to Staying in the Game

It's not enough to secure funding and create a budget — you also need to manage your finances carefully to ensure long-term success. Financial management is like keeping track of a team's performance over the course of a season. You need to monitor progress, adjust your tactics when necessary, and make sure that you're not burning out your resources too early in the game.

CASH FLOW MANAGEMENT

Cash flow is the lifeblood of your business. It's the equivalent of keeping your team hydrated during a game — if the cash runs out, the game is over. Managing cash flow involves keeping track of when money comes in and goes out of your business. You need to ensure that you have enough liquid assets to cover expenses while waiting for revenue to come in.

ACCOUNTS RECEIVABLE AND PAYABLE

Track your receivables (the money you're owed) and payables (the money you owe) closely. Just as a coach monitors player stats, you should regularly review your cash flow reports to spot any gaps or delays that could impact your ability to pay your bills or take advantage of growth opportunities.

FINANCIAL FORECASTING

Successful coaches always plan several games ahead. Similarly, financial forecasting involves predicting your business's future revenue, expenses, and cash flow. By forecasting, you can anticipate potential shortfalls and plan accordingly. Accurate forecasting allows you to make informed decisions about hiring, investments, and pricing strategies.

PROFITABILITY ANALYSIS

Keep a close eye on profitability — how much money your business is making after all expenses are paid. It's like reviewing your team's win-loss record: without regular assessments, you won't know if you're really succeeding. Understanding which products or services generate the most profit can help you prioritize your efforts and eliminate underperforming offerings.

DEBT MANAGEMENT

If your business has taken on loans or lines of credit, managing that debt is crucial. Just like a sports team that overextends its resources can find itself in trouble, a business that takes on too much debt risks financial collapse. Pay down high-interest debt first and avoid taking on more debt than your business can realistically handle.

TRACKING AND ADJUSTING: THE POST-GAME REVIEW

Just as a coach reviews game footage to make adjustments for future matches, you should regularly review your financial statements to assess the health of your business. This includes:

- Income statements: Show your revenue, expenses, and profit over a specific period, giving you insight into how well your business is performing.
- Balance sheets: Provide a snapshot of your assets, liabilities, and equity, showing you the overall financial strength of your business.
- Cash flow statements: Track the flow of cash in and out of your business, helping you manage liquidity and avoid cash shortages.

By regularly reviewing these financial reports, you can identify areas for improvement and make the necessary adjustments to keep your business on track.

Winning the Financial Game

In sports, it's often said that offense wins games, but defense wins championships. In business, having a solid financial strategy is your defense — protecting your business from financial risks and ensuring its long-term success. With proper funding, budgeting, and financial management, you'll have the resources and strategies necessary to not only stay in the game but to win it.

Sometimes the financial elements can overwhelm people. This is when it's good to have an expert strategic partner to help guide you, like a CPA. While partnering with such a professional can incur costs, they are usually well worth it. In my experience, a solid financial understanding is the difference in a smooth versus a bumpy ride forward.

Financial success isn't about making the most money in the shortest time; it's about building a sustainable business that can weather challenges, seize opportunities, and grow over the long term. With a strong financial foundation in place, you'll be ready to lead your business to victory.

Questions for You to Answer, Plus a Podcast Example to Consider

To start your business, do you know the answers to the following questions?

- How much money is a healthy amount of seed money to get started?
- Where will this money come from?
- What is the money used for?

Let's return to our podcast example and answer these questions.

How much money is a healthy amount of seed money to get started?

Having a weekly podcast produced for you will range from $15-30,000 per year. You could certainly produce the show yourself, but there will be a cost versus time versus experience analysis that may be required here. In addition, there is a need for the appropriate hardware, software, and various peripheral items to be successful. You not only need "the stuff" but if you're planning on doing visual recordings, you may need a professional-looking set for video recordings. This may range from $1-10,000 depending on the types of investments you choose to make in "your stuff."

Where will this money come from?

It is unlikely that you can get a business loan for a podcast alone. You may have to look to alternative means like personal savings, friends and family, or other sources. Perhaps a portion of each personal training session needs to be set aside for the first year of training to allow an accumulation of funds to execute on the podcast.

What is the money used for?

It seems like the answer would be that the majority of the funds will be used for the podcast and equipment. However, the reality is that the podcast is one area of focus among the three previously stated: as advertising for your services on your own show; as a guest expert on someone else's show to ultimately feed your business; and as a monetized content channel.

Once you invest money into resources like podcasting or other advertising, it is important to allow for two things. You have to give the plan some time to yield results, and you have to track those results. Any savvy advertising person will tell you that there is a lifecycle to advertising and marketing like this. If you want instant results, you might employ a different tactic than if you are developing a long-term online presence. Based on my knowledge of this space, consistency, time, and relevant content are the three ingredients to this recipe. If you are starting a podcast and doing it for a year, you need to rethink things. Unless you are a Hollywood star, your podcast isn't going to be successful in the first episode. This financial commitment likely needs to be for a sustainable period of time.

CHAPTER 9
LEGAL AND COMPLIANCE STRUCTURE

In sports, rules are crucial — they define how the game is played and what is allowed. Without rules, there's chaos. In business, the legal structure you choose acts like the rulebook, setting the framework for how your business will operate. From how you pay taxes to the level of liability you face, your legal structure impacts almost every aspect of your business. It's essential to choose the right legal structure for your goals.

Compliance, on the other hand, is about making sure you play by those rules. Just as a soccer team follows the rules of the game, your business must adhere to local, state, and federal regulations. Failing to comply with these regulations can lead to penalties, lawsuits, or even the dissolution of your business.

In this chapter, we will explore the various legal structures you can choose from and why maintaining compliance is critical to the long-term success of your business.

Choosing the Right Legal Structure: Building the Foundation

Each type of structure has its pros and cons, and choosing the wrong one can be costly. Here are the main types of legal structures to consider.

SOLE PROPRIETORSHIP

This is the simplest and most common structure, where you and the business are essentially one and the same.

- Advantages: Easy and inexpensive to set up, complete control over the business.
- Disadvantages: Unlimited personal liability, limited access to capital.

PARTNERSHIP

In a partnership, two or more people share ownership of the business. Partnerships can be general, where all partners share liability, or limited, where one partner has limited liability and involvement in the business.

- Advantages: Easy to establish, combined resources and skills, shared responsibility.
- Disadvantages: Joint and several liability, potential conflicts between partners.

LIMITED LIABILITY COMPANY (LLC)

An LLC is like building a solid defense for your business. It offers the flexibility of a partnership while providing limited liability protection to its owners, separating personal and business assets. This is like having both offensive and defensive players in place — protecting the business while allowing for growth and flexibility.

- Advantages: Limited liability protection, pass-through taxation, flexible management structure.
- Disadvantages: More complex and costly to form than sole proprietorship or partnership.

CORPORATION (C CORPORATION OR S CORPORATION)

A corporation is a separate legal entity from its owners, much like how a professional sports team is owned by shareholders and managed by a board of directors. The corporation structure offers the strongest personal liability protection, but it comes with more formalities and regulatory requirements.

- Advantages: Limited liability for shareholders, easier to raise capital, perpetual existence.
- Disadvantages: More expensive and complex to set up, double taxation (C Corporation), stricter compliance requirements.

NONPROFIT CORPORATION

If your business is focused on charitable, educational, or social causes, a nonprofit corporation might be the right choice. Nonprofits are similar to community-based sports programs, where the focus is on giving back, and any revenue is reinvested into the mission.

- Advantages: Tax-exempt status, eligibility for grants and donations.
- Disadvantages: Strict regulatory requirements, limited compensation for directors.

CHOOSING YOUR LEGAL STRUCTURE

You can choose a legal entity without considering financial or tax implications. However, taking a step back and looking at the bigger picture to harmonize the legal structure with the financial structure might make some sense. Time after time, I have represented small business owners that didn't know that a certain legal choice had a certain financial or tax impact, resulting in unwelcome surprises, like an unanticipated tax bill.

Whether this was due to a lack of understanding or a lack of information, it was a pain point that could have been avoided.

Lastly, legal structure may need to flex over time. This is really beyond the scope of this book, but I do want to acknowledge that most business owners have multiple entities that serve different purposes and achieve specific objectives. To get started, you need one entity, but it is reasonable to expect that you will add more as your business grows.

Understanding Compliance: Playing by the Rules

Once you've chosen your legal structure, the next step is ensuring compliance with laws and regulations. Think of compliance as the referee—keeping everyone in check and making sure the game is played fairly. Here are some compliance issues to keep in mind.

BUSINESS REGISTRATION AND LICENSING

Depending on your business structure and location, you may need to register with your state or local government. This is like signing up for the league. You'll need the right licenses or permits to operate legally. These vary by industry—some businesses need local permits (such as health permits for food service) while others might need federal licensing.

TAX OBLIGATIONS

The legal structure you choose affects how your business is taxed. A sole proprietor reports business income on their personal tax return, while corporations have separate tax filings. Make sure you know your tax obligations, including:

- Federal and state taxes. Understand the tax forms required based on your structure (e.g., Schedule C for sole proprietorships, Form 1120 for corporations).

- Sales tax. If you sell products, you may need to collect and remit sales tax.
- Payroll taxes. If you have employees, you're responsible for payroll taxes, including Social Security, Medicare, and unemployment taxes.

EMPLOYMENT LAWS

If you hire employees, you must comply with labor laws including wage requirements, worker safety, anti-discrimination policies, and benefits administration. This is like managing player contracts — each employee brings a set of legal responsibilities that you must honor.

ZONING AND ENVIRONMENTAL REGULATIONS

Depending on the nature of your business, zoning laws may restrict where you can operate. For instance, you can't open a noisy factory in a residential neighborhood without the proper permits. Similarly, if your business impacts the environment, you'll need to comply with environmental laws.

ONGOING FILINGS AND REPORTS

Some business structures, like corporations and LLCs, require you to file annual reports, hold regular meetings, and maintain accurate records of decisions. These formalities are like following team regulations — necessary for keeping your business in good standing.

The Role of Legal Counsel: Your Assistant Coach in Compliance and Risk Management

Just as every successful team has a coach, every successful business should have legal counsel. An experienced attorney can guide you through the complexities of business law, ensuring that you choose the right legal structure and remain compliant. Legal issues can arise unexpectedly, whether it's a contract dispute, employment law matter, or regulatory change. Having a legal professional on your team is crucial to ensuring that your business stays on the right side of the law.

I want my clients and my players to be well informed about the rules and regulations. This allows us to utilize the benefits of the rules and regulations while avoiding the pitfalls of the same. A lawyer can provide the expert insight needed to do just that.

This expertise can also be invaluable in risk management. While compliance is about playing by the rules, risk management is about anticipating potential problems and putting plans in place to avoid them. Every business faces risks — some you can predict, and others you can't. By identifying risks early and taking steps to mitigate them, you protect your business from costly penalties.

Beyond consulting an attorney on legal matters, risk mitigation planning can include:

- Insurance: Protect your business with the right insurance policies, such as general liability, professional liability, workers' compensation, and property insurance.
- Contracts: Use contracts to formalize relationships with vendors, clients, and employees. Clear, well-written contracts help prevent misunderstandings and disputes.
- Audits: Regularly reviewing your business practices and policies ensures that you remain compliant and minimizes the risk of violations.

Building a Strong, Legal Foundation

Just as a successful sports team requires discipline, strategy, and adherence to rules, a successful business requires a strong legal structure and commitment to compliance. By choosing the right legal structure, you set your business up for operational success, tax efficiency, and protection from liability. And by staying compliant with laws and regulations, you avoid penalties that could harm your business.

The running joke in the industry is that the attorney always says, "No, you can't do that." Professional ethics, risk mitigation, and sound business practices dictate that kind of answer. My best advice to entrepreneurs facing a "No" is to reframe the question. Tell your lawyer, "I'd like to achieve XYZ. How can I achieve that and minimize my risks in doing so, and *what is the cost of doing that*?" Yes, finance entered back into the equation.

Assume you have the time to do one of two tasks. Will you do the easy one or the hard one? Most gravitate to the easy; however, what if the easy results in cost to the business that outweighs the benefit? With your limited time, which decision creates the best return for the business considering all costs? You are starting to see how this decision tree can get a little complex. What if you don'tknow that answer? Again, your strategic partnerships can help you better understand the options and make the right choice for you.

Think of legal structure and compliance as the foundation for everything else in your business. With the right foundation in place, you can focus on growing your business, achieving your goals, and ultimately winning the game.

Questions for You to Answer, Plus a Podcast Example to Consider

Before getting started, make sure you are able to answer these questions:

- How should I organize my business?
- What risks do I have?
- How do I mitigate my risks in a cost-effective manner?

A fitness trainer's podcast has some flexibility on these answers.

How should I organize my business?

As a fitness trainer, your activities may dictate the need for the type of structure. If you're working for someone else, you don't need any of this stuff. However, if you are an independent contractor doing it on your own, having an entity separate from yourself will help with both risk and financial scenarios. Most likely an LLC is suitable for a startup fitness trainer. If that entity already exists, it might be appropriate to utilize its structure and contain the podcast within. However, in the event that you are attempting to monetize your content, a separate entity might be a useful tool to track the revenue streams differently.

What risks do I have?

Fitness trainers have some pretty big risks when working with people. Making sure folks are safe is paramount. However, a podcaster's risk is quite the opposite. There isn't a lot of true risk, absent being reckless or telling falsities. Misleading the public is the biggest risk, but if the comments are clearly stated and based in fact, it is tough to see how a podcast might harm someone.

How do I mitigate risks in a cost-effective manner?

Do your research and tell the truth. Although insurance could play a role here, it may not be necessary for a podcaster unless you own the facility or have employees. One of the great draws of content creation is the lack of risk. However, as we all know, sometimes the items that get the most attention are the most provocative, edgy, or controversial. This is not an endorsement of those extremes to push the boundaries, but simply an acknowledgment that you have some control over the risk you take on. Compared to the risk of keeping someone safe in a workout, podcast risk is minimal.

CHAPTER 10
PRODUCT OR SERVICE DEVELOPMENT

In sports, success depends on how well a team executes its game plan. For your business, success hinges on the quality of your product or service and how well it meets the needs of your customers. Just as a coach develops strategies and tactics for the team, you must continuously develop and refine your product or service to ensure it remains relevant and competitive.

Product or service development is at the core of your business. It's the reason customers engage with you, the value you deliver to them, and the foundation upon which your business is built. Whether you're creating something entirely new or improving an existing offering, the development process is essential for staying ahead of the competition and meeting market demands.\

In this chapter, we'll explore how to approach product or service development, from idea generation to execution, and why continuous improvement is key to maintaining a winning edge.

Understanding Your Market: Building Around Your Fans

Just as a coach must understand the strengths and weaknesses of the team's opponents, you need to understand your target market and the needs of your customers before developing your product or service. Customer insights are the foundation of successful product development. Without this understanding, you risk building something nobody wants or needs.

Start by answering these key questions:

1. Who are your customers? What are their demographics, behaviors, and pain points?
2. What problems are you solving? At its core, every product or service solves a problem for the customer. Identifying this problem and how your product addresses it is crucial.
3. What is the competition doing? Competitor analysis helps you understand the current landscape and what others in the market are offering.

The Development Process: Turning Ideas Into Reality

Product or service development is not a single-step process — it's a journey that involves several phases, each contributing to the refinement and execution of your idea. Here's how you can approach it:

IDEA GENERATION

This is where it all begins — brainstorming ideas for a new product or service, or ways to improve an existing one. Idea generation is all about creativity and thinking outside the box. Don't be afraid to gather input from different sources, including your team, customers, and industry trends.

PROTOTYPING AND TESTING

Once you have an idea, the next step is to create a prototype — a tangible or conceptual version of your product or service. During this stage, you'll want to test your product with real users to gather feedback and identify areas for improvement.

USER TESTING

User testing allows you to see how your product or service performs in the real world. This helps you identify any flaws or areas that need improvement before you go to market.

ITERATION AND REFINEMENT

Based on the feedback you receive, you'll need to refine and improve your product or service. Continuous improvement is key to developing a product that truly meets the needs of your customers.

FINAL PRODUCT DEVELOPMENT

After several iterations, you'll be ready to finalize your product or service for launch. This is like a team putting all the elements together before game day—every piece should be in place to ensure a smooth and successful launch.

Balancing Innovation with Practicality

In sports, innovation can be the difference between winning and losing, but it needs to be balanced with practicality. The same applies to product development. You want to create something innovative, but it also needs to be feasible to produce and deliver. That means considering cost-effectiveness and scalability.

Ensure that the costs associated with developing and delivering your product or service align with your pricing strategy. Over-engineering a product might make it expensive and less attractive to your target market.

Additionally, consider whether your product or service can scale as your business grows. You need to plan for how your offering can be expanded or adapted as demand increases. If your product or service can't grow with your business, you may face limitations down the road.

Customer Feedback: Your Real-Time Playbook

Customers are the best source of insight into how well your product is meeting their needs and how you can enhance it. Gather feedback regularly, encouraging customers to share their experiences with your product or service. This can be done through surveys, reviews, or direct communication.

Then act on that feedback. Whether it's addressing bugs in a product or tweaking your service delivery process, making continuous improvements ensures that you stay competitive and keep your customers happy.

Product or service development is an ongoing process, and you should always be thinking about how to enhance your offerings and stay ahead of competitors. This could involve anything from adding new features and entering new markets to exploring new technologies. It's not enough to launch a great product or service — you need to keep refining it to ensure that it remains the best solution for your customers.

Crafting a Winning Product or Service

Product or service development is at the heart of every successful business. Just as a winning team is built on the strength of its players and strategy, your business is built on the quality of the products or services you offer. By understanding your customers, refining your ideas, and continuously improving, you can create offerings that stand out in the market, and keep your customers coming back for more.

Success doesn't come from just one great play. It comes from a well-executed game plan, constant improvement, and a commitment to excellence. With the right approach to product or service development, your business can achieve lasting success and build a loyal customer base that believes in your vision. If you develop your vision enough, you know what to do, even when you don't know what to do!

Questions for You to Answer, Plus a Podcast Example to Consider

Developing a winning product or service requires doing your research and investing in what you know. So, what is it that you know?

- How does this skill make things better or solve a problem for other people?
- How much do I think that is worth to someone else?
- What adjustments to my offering need to be made?

Again, let's consider what a fitness trainer might be able to offer someone in a podcast setting:

What do you know?

The fitness trainer has both knowledge and experience with both the human body and mind. Combining both physical activity and mental toughness is necessary during workouts, periods of rest, and in committing to a healthy diet. A podcast would be an easy and duplicatable message to reach as many people as possible about the various messages and techniques that the trainer has found effective in training clients over the years.

How does this skill make things better or solve a problem for other people?

A trainer can't be with a client more than a few hours a week. You might have one to three hours a week with a client. Podcasts and their recordings could supplement this limited time together. Many people struggle with the accountability of health and fitness in their busy lifestyles. Perhaps helping people be more accountable without being present is an incredibly valuable tool. It seems to work for companies like Peloton.

How much do you think the podcast is worth to someone else?

Initially, the podcast is likely a lead generation tool or a free "add on" to help a trainer stand out from other trainers. However, there is a case where the free version of the broadcast and recordings are only the tip of the iceberg. Maybe there needs to be a monthly subscription model allowing current clients more structured health and fitness information. This subscription could be tiered, with one level for clients at a discounted rate and a full price model for non-clients. Ultimately, pricing is in the hands of the consumer.

What adjustments to the offering are needed?

This is likely the result of conversations with folks and requesting feedback over time. I would focus first on the free version of the podcast to reach as many people as possible as well as on building a library of recorded content for the future. While developing these episodes, pay attention to comments, feedback, and other interactions based on the subjects so you can identify opportunities for deeper dives into topics with which the audience engages more.

CHAPTER 11
BRANDING AND MARKETING

In sports, a team's identity is often defined by its logo, colors, and the way it plays. This identity builds loyalty among fans and creates a strong presence both on and off the field. In business, your brand is your identity. It represents who you are, what you stand for, and how you are perceived in the market. A strong brand builds trust with your customers, differentiates you from the competition, and creates lasting connections.

Marketing is the process of communicating that brand identity to the world. Just as a sports team promotes itself to attract fans and sponsors, your business needs marketing strategies to attract customers, build awareness, and foster loyalty. Branding and marketing work hand in hand, helping your business create a memorable identity and communicate it effectively.

In this chapter, we'll explore how to develop a strong brand and implement marketing strategies that engage your target audience and drive growth.

What is Branding? Defining Your Identity

Your brand is more than just a logo or a tagline — it's the essence of your business. It's how you want your customers to feel when they think of your company, the promise you make to them, and the values you stand for. A powerful brand is consistent, clear, and easily recognizable.

BRAND VALUES AND MISSION

What does your business stand for? Much like a sports team's mission to win championships or inspire a community, your brand's values and mission should reflect your goals and the purpose of your business. These values will guide how you operate and how you connect with your customers.

BRAND VOICE AND PERSONALITY

The tone and personality of your brand are crucial to how customers perceive you. Are you professional, friendly, innovative, or quirky? Defining your brand's voice helps ensure that every interaction with customers — whether through marketing materials, social media, or customer service — is consistent and aligned with your identity.

VISUAL IDENTITY

This includes your logo, color palette, typography, and overall visual style. Your visual branding should be unique and memorable. Strong visual branding helps you stand out in a crowded marketplace and makes it easy for customers to identify your business at a glance.

The Role of Marketing: Spreading the Word

Once you've defined your brand, marketing is the tool you use to communicate it to your audience. It's about building awareness, generating leads, and converting them into loyal customers. Here are key elements of a strong marketing strategy:

TARGET AUDIENCE

Who are your ideal customers? What are their needs, preferences, and pain points? Knowing your audience allows you to create messaging that resonates with them and addresses their specific concerns.

VALUE PROPOSITION

Your value proposition is the unique benefit that your product or service provides. Why should customers choose your business over competitors?

MARKETING CHANNELS

There are many ways to reach your audience, from traditional methods like print advertising and direct mail to digital platforms like social media, email marketing, and search engine optimization (SEO). It's important to choose the channels that best suit your audience. Meet your customers where they are.

Creating a Memorable Brand Experience

In sports, it's not just about the game — it's about the entire experience, from the stadium atmosphere to the interactions with fans. Your business should aim to create a memorable brand experience that resonates with customers at every touchpoint. This is what fosters loyalty and turns one-time customers into lifelong supporters. Here are some ways to do that.

CONSISTENCY ACROSS TOUCHPOINTS

Ensure that your brand is consistent across all customer interactions, from your website and social media to customer service and in-store experience. Just as a team maintains its identity across different arenas, your brand should be instantly recognizable no matter how customers interact with you.

CUSTOMER ENGAGEMENT

Engaging with customers is like engaging with fans. Respond to feedback, engage on social media, and create opportunities for customers to interact with your brand. A loyal fan base doesn't just watch games — they participate in the experience, and you want your customers to do the same with your business.

STORYTELLING

Storytelling is a powerful tool in both sports and business. Every successful team has a story — whether it's a long history of championships or an underdog journey. Your business should have a story too — something that customers can connect with and that sets you apart. Share the story of how your business was founded, what your mission is, or the impact you've made.

Digital Marketing: The Modern Playing Field

In today's world, digital marketing is the dominant playing field for most businesses. It allows you to reach a large audience, track the effectiveness of your campaigns, and engage with customers in real time. Much like how sports teams use social media to connect with fans, your business should leverage digital marketing to build and maintain relationships with customers. Examples include:

- Social media. Platforms like Facebook, Instagram, LinkedIn, and Twitter are essential for building brand awareness and engaging with customers. Use social media to share updates, run promotions, and interact with your audience.
- Content marketing. Content marketing involves creating valuable, relevant content to attract and engage your target audience. This could be through blog posts, videos, infographics, or eBooks.
- Email marketing. Email marketing remains one of the most effective ways to nurture leads and maintain relationships with customers. Regularly sending newsletters or promotional offers keeps your customers informed and engaged.
- SEO and paid advertising. Optimizing your website for search engines (SEO) ensures that customers can find you when they search for products or services related to your

business. Paid advertising, such as Google Ads or social media ads, allows you to reach a broader audience quickly.

Brand Loyalty: Building Long-Term Relationships

In sports, a team's success isn't just measured by wins but by the loyalty of its fans. Similarly, a successful business isn't just about one-time sales—it's about building long-term relationships with customers. Brand loyalty is earned through trust, consistency, and delivering value over time.

Just as teams work hard to keep fans coming back season after season, your business should focus on retaining customers. This involves delivering on your promises, providing excellent customer service, and continuously improving your products or services.

Consider implementing loyalty programs or rewards for repeat customers. These programs incentivize customers to stay engaged with your brand and keep coming back, much like season ticket holders in sports.

Finally, encourage your customers to become advocates for your brand. Creating a sense of community around your brand—whether through social media groups, events, or customer spotlights—can turn satisfied customers into enthusiastic supporters who spread the word about your business.

Crafting a Brand That Wins

Coca-Cola is a beautiful example of a brand that needs no introduction. Simply by seeing the font and colors, you know. Whether the can is red, white, or black, you know. Over the years this company has spent mountains of money on their marketing and branding. Needless to say, as a startup, you are not going to be in this league. However, you can keep this concept in mind as you think about your customer experience.

Building a strong brand and marketing it effectively is essential to the success of your business. Just like a sports team, your business needs a clear identity, loyal supporters, and a strategy for engaging with your audience. By defining your brand, creating a memorable experience, and using effective marketing strategies, you can build lasting relationships with customers and stand out in a competitive marketplace.

Remember, success in branding and marketing doesn't happen overnight — it's built over time through consistent effort, creativity, and a deep understanding of your audience. With the right approach, your business can cultivate a brand that wins not just today, but for years to come.

Questions for You to Answer, Plus a Podcast Example to Consider

Let's reflect on a mission, vision, and value statement to determine the following:

- What message do I want to send my audience?
- Do I have a story to convey to my audience?
- How will my customers remember my product or service?
- What is the actionable item that should happen when seeing "my stuff?"

A fitness trainer's mission, vision, and value statements might be vastly different, but let's borrow a real-life example to help answer these questions.

Peloton is a well-respected fitness company across the globe. The following quotes are taken from their website. Their stated mission is, "bring integrated fitness and wellness experiences to members anytime, anywhere." Their values are: believe, bring your best, and lift people up. Their stated purpose, which I'll adjust to vision, is to "empower people to live fit, strong, long and happy lives."

Let's assume our fitness trainer has a similar philosophy.

What message do you want to send your audience?

The podcast and supporting materials need to convey a message to the client that they can engage in a way that improves your health and fitness goals. You are a facilitator, aiding the person to achieve their health and fitness objectives, and you have a set of tools and skill set that makes it easier for the client to meet this objective.

Do you have a story to convey to your audience?

You better! Sometimes the story may be as simple as, "I'm successful when you are successful. Therefore, I am here to support your success." Maybe there are a series of sub-stories that you can tell to relate and/or personalize the experience for folks. Client testimonial stories relaying how the trainer impacted someone's life and helped them overcome a pain point could be useful.

How do you think the customers will remember your product or service?

Hopefully, there is a sense of motivation and accomplishment that gets conveyed from the podcast to its listeners. The trainer wants the audience to feel as if they can accomplish their objectives and take next steps to do exactly that. If done properly, the audience will more deeply engage with the podcast and the trainer, and ultimately buy more classes or subscriptions.

What's the actionable item that should happen when seeing "your stuff?"

Whatever the promotional material, the trainer will want the audience to feel motivated and engaged to keep developing their fitness journey. Ideally, the listener turns into a client in some form; however, there are ancillary benefits of people simply enjoying and sharing your content.

CHAPTER 12
SALES STRATEGY

In sports, no matter how good the team is at defense, if they don't score goals, they can't win the game. In business, sales are your goals. Without sales, your business can't succeed. Your sales strategy is your game plan for driving revenue, attracting customers, and growing your business. It's the blueprint for how you will turn potential leads into loyal customers.

Just like a coach prepares the team with offensive strategies to score, you need a well-defined sales strategy to ensure your business can generate consistent revenue and thrive in the marketplace. This chapter will guide you through the key components of a winning sales strategy, helping you define your approach to closing deals and achieving long-term success.

Understanding Your Sales Funnel: From Leads to Loyal Customers

A sales funnel represents the journey a potential customer takes from first learning about your business to making a purchase and beyond. It filters prospects through different stages, and only some make it to the final purchase. Here's how the sales funnel breaks down:

- Awareness: This is the top of the funnel where potential customers first become aware of your brand. In this stage, your goal is to attract attention and spark interest through marketing efforts.

- Interest: Once prospects know who you are, the next step is getting them interested in your product or service. They are beginning to evaluate whether your offering can solve their problem.
- Decision: At this stage, prospects are actively deciding whether to purchase from you or a competitor. Your goal here is to provide compelling reasons — such as unique value propositions, pricing, or guarantees — to choose your business.
- Action: The final stage is when the prospect makes a purchase, turning them into a customer.
- Retention and Loyalty: Just as a team wants fans to keep coming back to games, you want your customers to return for repeat business. Building customer loyalty through follow-ups, excellent service, and continued engagement is critical for long-term success.

Developing Your Sales Playbook

Much like a team relies on a playbook to execute successful strategies on the field, your sales strategy should be structured and well-defined. Every business's sales strategy will vary depending on its industry, market, and target customers, but there are some universal components to consider:

DEFINE YOUR SALES PROCESS

A clear, repeatable sales process is essential for closing deals. Your process should outline the specific steps your sales team takes from lead generation to closing a sale. This might include initial outreach, product demonstrations, addressing objections, and negotiating terms. The more structured your sales process, the easier it will be to train your team and track progress.

IDENTIFY YOUR UNIQUE SELLING PROPOSITION (USP)

Just like a sports team needs a signature play or style to stand out, your business needs a unique selling proposition. Your USP is the key reason why customers should choose your product or service over competitors. Is it your quality, price, speed, or customer service? Identifying and communicating your USP effectively can make the difference in closing a sale.

LEAD GENERATION STRATEGY

Generating leads is like recruiting players for a team. You need to have a steady pipeline of potential customers to keep your sales moving. Whether you use content marketing, social media advertising, email campaigns, or cold outreach, it's important to have a strategy for continually bringing new leads into your sales funnel.

NURTURING LEADS

Not every lead is ready to make an immediate purchase. Just like a coach helps develop young players over time, you need to nurture leads until they are ready to buy. This can be done through regular communication, offering valuable content, or answering their questions and concerns.

CLOSING THE DEAL

This is where your sales team must excel. Closing requires the right combination of timing, negotiation, and persuasion. Much like a striker needs to time their shot perfectly, your sales team needs to know when to push for a close without being too aggressive or losing the prospect's trust.

Pricing Strategy: Finding the Sweet Spot

Pricing is a critical element of your sales strategy. Set your prices too high, and you risk alienating potential customers; set them too low, and you might undervalue your offering or hurt your profit margins. Pricing is like balancing the offense and defense in a game — you need to find the right mix to be successful. There are a few pricing strategies you might try.

COST-PLUS PRICING

This method involves calculating the cost of producing your product or delivering your service and then adding a markup. It's a straightforward approach but may not account for market conditions or customer willingness to pay.

COMPETITIVE PRICING

In this strategy, you set your prices based on what your competitors are charging. It's like watching other teams to see how they play and adjusting your strategy accordingly. This method ensures that you stay competitive, but it may not highlight the unique value of your product.

VALUE-BASED PRICING

Value-based pricing involves setting your prices based on the perceived value to the customer rather than your costs. This is like a star player commanding a high salary because of their contribution to the team's success. If your product or service delivers significant value, customers may be willing to pay a premium.

DISCOUNTS AND PROMOTIONS

Offering discounts and promotions can help attract customers and drive short-term sales, but be cautious not to rely too heavily on discounts, as it can devalue your brand. Think of promotions like limited-time offers in sports — strategic use can generate excitement, but overuse can lower value.

Leveraging Technology in Sales

Technology has revolutionized how businesses approach sales. Leveraging sales software and digital tools can improve efficiency, track performance, and help you close deals faster.

For example, customer relationship management (CRM) systems help manage interactions with current and potential customers. With CRM software, you can keep track of leads, follow up on opportunities, and manage customer relationships more effectively.

There are also sales automation tools. Automating certain parts of the sales process, such as email follow-ups or lead scoring, allows your sales team to focus on high-value tasks like building relationships and closing deals. Automation ensures that nothing falls through the cracks, just as coaches rely on systems to track player performance and game statistics.

Finally, there's data analytics. Analyzing sales data helps you identify patterns, optimize your sales process, and make informed decisions. Just as teams use analytics to determine which plays are most effective, your sales team can use data to understand which approaches work best and how to improve overall performance.

Playing to Win in Sales

If you offer a service or a good that is needed, you do not have to sell it. That sounds too good to be true, right? You have to be out there, offering the goods or services to the right people at the right time. A strong sales strategy is the key to driving revenue and growing your business. Just like in sports, success comes from having a clear game plan, executing it well, and continuously improving over time.

Remember, sales is not just about closing deals. It's about building relationships, understanding your customers' needs, and delivering value. With the right strategy in place, your business can score the goals that matter and keep winning for years to come.

Questions for You to Answer, Plus a Podcast Example to Consider

When developing your sales strategy, ask yourself these questions:

- Do I have something to offer that is truly desired?
- Who will I reach out to first?
- Do I have a system to foster people through the awareness, interest, decision, action, and retention cycles?
- Who will undertake this effort?

Now, let's consider those questions in the context of our fitness instructor turned podcaster.

Do you have something to offer that is truly desired?

Our fitness trainer absolutely has something that people want. Remember, health and fitness is a $22.4 billion industry.[6] The issue here is how you can convince someone to use you and *your* methods over others. What about content on the podcast? I would start with finding ways to share information from already validated resources to boost your credibility. Maybe having doctors, athletes, or coaches as guests can compel more listeners.

---

6 Health & Fitness Association Staff, "The U.S. Health and Fitness Industry Is a $22.4 Billion Economic Powerhouse," Health & Fitness Association, May 7, 2024, https://www.healthandfitness.org/about/media-center/press-releases/the-health-and-fitness-industry-is-22-4-billion-economic-powerhouse-3/.

Who will you reach out to first?

Oftentimes, word of mouth is the cheapest and most effective way of getting people to work with you. You could always ask for your closest friends and family to serve as a platform for your message. There are also opportunities to host and participate in fitness events in your community to help expand your brand's presence.

Do you have a system to foster people through the awareness, interest, decision, action, and retention cycles?

Making someone aware that you're in the business is one thing, but getting them to pay you for services is another. This is where the power of a pre-determined system can help engage folks. Giving a business card and stopping there is going to yield a different result than following up with someone after exchanging info. Giving away a "free session" to someone who subscribed to your podcast might help create the engagement needed to evolve from awareness to action. Most importantly, you want repeat customers, so you need to consider developing something that will compel repetitive action. The podcast can hit on all five of these elements by weaving in interaction through unique guests, giveaways, promotions, and more, ultimately ensuring the listener gets what they need at each step of the process.

Who will undertake this effort?

If you are a business of one, you are the one who has to shoulder this burden. Initially our fitness coach will be the one executing on these steps. Joining a networking group would be a smart call. Not only could this be a group of listeners but a source of feedback, and perhaps a passive marketing team.

Once there is an advertising budget, you can execute this objective differently. Many in this space focus on targeted advertising because this immediately focuses on step two.

Targeted advertising focuses on those that are already interested and sometimes searching or working toward deciding to take action. In the right environment, you can collapse awareness, interest, and decision into a singular process. Placing a targeted ad on Facebook that appears when someone is scrolling content related to health and fitness is the objective. Now you have to focus on action and retention only.

CHAPTER 13
TEAM BUILDING

In any successful sports team, victory isn't achieved by one star player alone. It's the result of the combined efforts of every member working together. In business, the same principle applies: Building a strong, cohesive team is essential to reaching your goals and driving your company's success. Your team is the engine behind your business, and the stronger it is, the more capable your business will be at achieving long-term success.

Whether you're hiring your first employees or expanding an existing crew, team building is about creating a group of individuals who bring diverse skills, ideas, and perspectives to the table but who are united by a shared purpose. In this chapter, you will explore how to build a strong, effective team that works together to drive your business forward.

Defining the Roles: Putting the Right Players in the Right Positions

Just as a coach assigns players to positions based on their strengths, building a successful business team starts with defining clear roles. Understanding the specific needs of your business and matching those needs with the right individuals is key to building a strong team. This is about getting the right people in the right roles — whether it's finding a marketing expert, a tech guru, or a sales superstar.

ASSESS YOUR NEEDS

Start by assessing what your business needs in terms of skills, expertise, and capabilities. What gaps exist in your current operations? Do you need technical experts, creative thinkers, or sales professionals? Identifying these needs will guide you as you build your team.

JOB DESCRIPTIONS

Once you've assessed your needs, create detailed job descriptions for each role. Just like each player on a sports team has a specific position with responsibilities, your employees should have clearly defined roles so they understand their responsibilities and how they contribute to the business's success.

MATCH SKILLS TO ROLES

Not every employee fits neatly into one role. You may need individuals who can wear multiple hats or who bring a diverse set of skills to the table. When hiring, look for candidates whose strengths align with your needs, but who can also grow with the company and take on additional responsibilities as needed.

Recruiting Talent: Building a High-Performance Team

Recruiting the right talent is a crucial step in team building. In sports, coaches look for players who have not only the necessary skills but also the right attitude and chemistry to fit within the team. Similarly, recruiting for your business should focus not only on qualifications but also on cultural fit, mindset, and long-term potential.

CREATE AN ATTRACTIVE EMPLOYER BRAND

The best talent is attracted to companies that offer more than just a paycheck. Building a strong employer brand — one that reflects your company's values, culture, and mission — helps attract candidates who align with your vision. Just as sports teams create a winning culture that attracts star players, your business should create a culture that appeals to top talent.

USE MULTIPLE CHANNELS

To find the best candidates, use a variety of recruiting channels. This could include online job boards, social media, employee referrals, and recruitment agencies. Just as a sports team scouts players from various leagues, you should cast a wide net to attract diverse talent.

FOCUS ON CULTURAL FIT

Skills and experience are important, but so is cultural fit. Hiring employees who align with your company's values and culture ensures that your team works well together and shares a common vision. In sports, team chemistry can make or break a season — the same holds true for your business.

CONSIDER FUTURE GROWTH

When recruiting, think not only about your current needs but also about the future. Will the candidate be able to grow with the company? Are they adaptable and willing to take on new challenges? Look for individuals who are skilled and flexible and open to growth.

Fostering Teamwork: Building a Culture of Collaboration

Once you've assembled your team, fostering a culture of collaboration is key to ensuring that everyone works well together. In sports, a team that doesn't communicate or collaborate will struggle to succeed, no matter how talented the individual players are. The same is true in business. Here are some ways to create a culture where teamwork is valued and fostered.

ENCOURAGE OPEN COMMUNICATION

Open communication is the foundation of effective teamwork. Encourage your team to share ideas, give feedback, and voice concerns. Just as a coach fosters communication between players during a game, you should create an environment where employees feel comfortable speaking up and contributing.

PROMOTE COLLABORATION

Collaboration is more than just working together — it's about leveraging each team member's strengths to achieve a common goal. Encourage cross-functional collaboration, where employees from different departments or areas of expertise work together on projects. This not only fosters innovation but also strengthens relationships within the team.

SET CLEAR GOALS AND EXPECTATIONS

Just as a coach sets goals for the team, you should set clear goals and expectations for your employees. This gives them a sense of direction and purpose and ensures that everyone is working toward the same objectives. Clearly defined goals also provide a framework for measuring progress and celebrating achievements.

CELEBRATE WINS AS A TEAM

Just as sports teams celebrate their victories together, it's important to celebrate wins with your team. Whether it's reaching a milestone, completing a successful project, or achieving company-wide goals, celebrating successes fosters a sense of unity and accomplishment.

Training and Development: Continuously Improving the Team

Great teams don't stop training after the season starts — they are always looking for ways to improve. The same applies to your business team. Continuous learning and development are essential for keeping your employees engaged, improving their skills, and helping them grow within the company. The following options can provide improvement opportunities for your team.

- Training programs: Invest in training programs that help your employees develop new skills and stay up to date with industry trends. This could include workshops, seminars, online courses, or mentorship programs.
- Professional development: Encourage your team to pursue professional development opportunities, whether it's earning certifications, attending industry conferences, or learning new technologies. Supporting their growth benefits the individual and strengthens the team.
- Regular feedback: Provide regular, constructive feedback to your employees. This helps them understand what they're doing well and where they can improve.
- Promotions from within: Rewarding hard work and promoting from within builds trust and loyalty within your team. Offering growth opportunities shows that you value employees' contributions and are invested in their future with the company.

Building Trust and Accountability

Building trust within your team is essential to creating a high-performance culture. Trust starts at the top. As a leader, you set the tone for the rest of the team. Demonstrate integrity, accountability, and transparency in your actions, and your team will follow suit. Just as a captain leads the team on the field, your leadership sets the standard for the business.

Accountability is also key to building trust within a team. Hold everyone, including yourself, accountable for meeting goals, fulfilling responsibilities, and maintaining a high standard of work. When employees know that everyone is held to the same standards, they are more likely to trust each other and work together effectively.

Finally, foster a safe environment. Create an environment where employees feel safe to take risks, make mistakes, and learn from them. Just as a coach allows players to take risks on the field, you should encourage innovation and experimentation within your team. This fosters creativity and growth, while building trust among team members.

Building a Team That Wins

The team is only as strong as the weakest link. Building a strong team is one of the most important factors in the success of your business. Just like a sports team needs the right players, strategy, and leadership to win, your business needs the right people working together toward a common goal. By defining roles, recruiting top talent, fostering collaboration, and continuously developing your team, you can create a high-performance culture that drives success.

If you empower your people to succeed in their various roles, you will see successes beyond anticipation. How do you do this? You start with a clear expectation of the goal. "Win at all costs" might convey the message that we will cheat or otherwise take steps outside of the rules to achieve a win. "Win with respect and integrity" may yield a different result. Choose your words wisely as you motivate your team. Think strategically and consider the idea that most people remember how you made them feel, not what you did.

Again, building a winning team is not a one-time effort. It's an ongoing process of growth, learning, and improvement. With the right approach to team building, your business can achieve great things and create a legacy of success.

Questions for You to Answer, Plus a Podcast Example to Consider

Here are some questions to think about when building your team:

- Who are the players I want on my team?
- Can I expand on the team's skill sets?
- Do I have clear objectives for a role?

Now, let's answer those questions with our fitness instructor turned podcaster in mind.

Who are the players I want on my team?

When you start, you're it. As the podcast fills all the training spots, you may need to get another trainer. A male trainer may want to hire a female trainer to bring in a balance of masculine and feminine qualities into the business.

Before you "grow" for the money, it is important to think about how that growth may need support. Podcasts can have a lot of formats and an endless number of guests and/or co-hosts. Since the podcast was a tool to develop both marketing leads and internal content, it might make sense to target someone with virtual skills and/or education training in addition to their skills in the health and fitness industry.

Having an idea of where you are headed and who you should hire is key, so when you are starting out, having some metrics in place to know when to revisit this initiative is helpful. For example, "When I have thirty sessions per week booked, I need to start looking for someone to assist me."

Can I expand on the team's skill sets?

As a fitness trainer, you have the physical part down. Maybe you are good with the fundamentals of nutrition, but you're not a specialist. If you had a teammate that specializes in nutrition, you can both achieve goals together you couldn't on your own. Once you have a person in the role, you should work together to expand based on their strengths to create new lines of revenue while ensuring continued fulfillment.

Do I have clear objectives for a role?

At this point the questions and answers may feel a little muddy. That is intentional: I've tried to mix up what our fitness trainer needs on purpose. You will be faced with the same problems: "I need help, I can't do it all on my own!" But who do you hire and what do you give away to that new hire?

Most likely the fitness trainer will not hire someone to replace the podcast efforts. The new hire can be a guest or periodically substitute as host, but if the brand is built around the host's personality and message, that needs to be consistent. In reality you are hiring another trainer to help take on more customers or a specialist to help develop a line of services that you couldn't do otherwise. Having a proper nutrition plan is essential to a healthy lifestyle, but frequently nutritionists are focused on a specific need. Although that may seem attractive, is it a core in-house need? Perhaps our fitness trainer should focus solely on what got them to this point: fitness training and classes. The key is finding someone who can bring consistency and a layer of diversity to the already established and growing training business.

CHAPTER 14
TECHNOLOGY AND INFRASTRUCTURE

In sports, a team's success depends not only on the players and the coach but also on the training facilities, equipment, and technology that supports them. Similarly, in business, technology and infrastructure serve as the backbone that enables your team to perform at its best. A solid technological foundation allows your business to operate efficiently, scale effectively, and compete in today's fast-paced digital world.

Technology and infrastructure are the tools and systems that keep your business running smoothly. From the hardware and software that power your operations to the cloud services that store your data, the right infrastructure ensures your business can meet customer demands, adapt to change, and grow sustainably. In this chapter, we will explore how to build and maintain a strong technological infrastructure that supports your business goals.

Understanding Your Business's Technological Needs

Before investing in technology, it's important to understand what your business needs to operate efficiently and scale. Just as a sports team assesses its needs for training facilities, fitness equipment, and game-day technology, your business should assess its needs in terms of hardware, software, and systems.

ASSESSING YOUR OPERATIONS

Start by assessing your current operations. What processes are in place, and how are they managed? Are there manual tasks that could be automated? Identifying inefficiencies in your existing operations will help you determine where technology can make the biggest impact.

IDENTIFYING KEY AREAS

Determine the key areas where technology is critical to your business's success. This could include areas such as sales, marketing, customer service, inventory management, or finance. Each department may have different needs, and your technology infrastructure should address those needs accordingly.

SCALABILITY

Think about the future. As your business grows, will your current technology systems be able to scale with you? Just as a team needs to plan for future seasons, your business needs to invest in technology that can grow and adapt to increased demand and complexity.

Building the Right Infrastructure: Hardware, Software, and Systems

Once you've identified your business's needs, the next step is building the right infrastructure. This includes choosing the right hardware, software, and systems that will support your business and its goals.

- Hardware: The physical equipment that powers your business is just as important as the people who use it. This includes computers, servers, networking devices, and any specialized equipment needed for your industry.
- Software: Software is the engine that drives your business processes. From CRM systems to accounting software, the

right tools can streamline operations, improve productivity, and enhance customer satisfaction.
- Cloud Services: Cloud computing has revolutionized how businesses store and manage data. By moving to the cloud, you can access your business's data and applications from anywhere, scale quickly, and reduce costs associated with maintaining physical servers.
- Cybersecurity: Cybersecurity solutions protect your business data, systems, and intellectual property. Invest in firewalls, antivirus software, encryption, and employee training to safeguard your business from cyber threats.

Evaluate hardware, software, and systems options based on your business's specific needs. For example, when it comes to software, are you looking for tools to manage customer interactions, track inventory, or process payroll? Make sure the tool you choose is easy to use, integrates with your existing systems, and offers the features you need.

Integrating Technology into Your Business Operations

Technology isn't just about having the latest gadgets — it's about how you integrate those tools into your day-to-day operations. A well-planned integration of technology can boost efficiency, reduce costs, and improve customer satisfaction.

AUTOMATING PROCESSES

Automation is one of the most powerful ways to increase efficiency in your business. By automating repetitive tasks such as invoicing, inventory tracking, and customer communication, you can free up your team to focus on more strategic activities. Think of automation as streamlining your plays — it removes unnecessary steps and helps your team execute faster and more efficiently.

DATA MANAGEMENT AND ANALYTICS

In sports, coaches rely on data analytics to make informed decisions about game strategy and player performance. In business, data is just as important. Implement systems that allow you to collect, store, and analyze data from across your operations. This data can provide valuable insights into customer behavior, sales trends, and operational efficiencies, helping you make more informed decisions.

IMPROVING COMMUNICATION

Effective communication is the key to any successful team, and technology plays a crucial role in enabling communication across your business. Invest in tools that allow your team to collaborate in real time, whether they're in the office or working remotely. This includes video conferencing software, project management platforms, and instant messaging tools.

Supporting Remote Work and Flexibility

The rise of remote work has made flexible working arrangements an essential part of modern business. Technology plays a crucial role in enabling remote work, ensuring that your team remains productive and connected no matter where they are.

REMOTE ACCESS TO SYSTEMS

Ensure that your employees can access the systems and tools they need to do their jobs from any location. This may involve using cloud-based software, virtual private networks (VPNs), or remote desktop solutions to provide secure access to your business's data and applications.

COLLABORATION TOOLS

Remote work requires seamless communication and collaboration between team members. Invest in tools like Slack, Microsoft Teams, or Zoom to facilitate real-time communication, project management, and collaboration on documents. These tools ensure that your team stays connected and productive, no matter where they're working.

MAINTAINING SECURITY

Remote work also introduces new security challenges, as employees access sensitive data from outside the office. Implement strong security protocols, such as two-factor authentication, encryption, and secure Wi-Fi networks, to protect your business's data when employees are working remotely.

Maintaining and Updating Your Infrastructure

Technology is constantly evolving, and your business needs to keep up with these changes to remain competitive. Just as a team continuously trains and updates its strategies, your business should regularly evaluate and update its technology and infrastructure.

Schedule regular maintenance for your hardware, software, and systems to ensure they are functioning properly. This includes updating software, backing up data, and replacing outdated equipment. Neglecting maintenance can lead to costly downtime and lost productivity.

As your business grows, your technology needs will change. Be proactive in upgrading your systems to handle increased demand, improve performance, and take advantage of new features. Regularly assess whether your current infrastructure is meeting your business's needs, and be prepared to invest in new technology when necessary.

Finally, technology is constantly advancing, and new tools and solutions are being developed every day. Stay informed about industry trends, emerging technologies, and best practices by attending conferences, reading industry publications, and networking with peers. Being aware of the latest innovations can help your business stay ahead of the competition.

The System v. The Business: Technology Is Just One Player

As a coach, I try to be mindful of my player utilization. In tournaments, it is important to rest key players during the earlier matches, so they have more in reserve for matches later in the day. In modern soccer, players can wear trackers that help monitor distance travelled to help manage their fitness levels and prevent overuse. Or you can simply use a stopwatch and monitor playing time to achieve a similar goal. Both methods may achieve the same objective, but one is more costly and accurate whereas the other is cheaper but less accurate.

You will be faced with similar decisions when deciding what technologies to incorporate into your business. I once represented a business owner who was a master of all the tools of his craft. He had everything set up to precisely measure, track, and identify his customers from initial contact through the close of business in his sales cycle. He even had integrations from different software sources to automate the accounting and tax process. It might have been the most sophisticated system I saw in his industry. What's the catch, you ask? The system is only as good as the data it contains.

In this example, he had lots of leads, many of which were not ripe or legitimate leads. The focus on the system was so acute that he forgot the bigger picture. The system was perfect, but there were not enough viable sales in the system to justify it. Leads did not convert into customers without someone putting in the time to make that happen. The system could not do it for him. Having technology systems and tools are essential to optimizing your business, but do not forget you have to run both the business and the technology, too.

By investing in the right tools, integrating them into your operations, and continuously maintaining and upgrading your systems, you can build a solid technological foundation that supports your business's growth and success. Technology is not just a support function — it's a key player in your business's success. With the right infrastructure in place, your business can operate more efficiently, respond to customer needs more quickly, and stay ahead of the competition in today's fast-paced market.

Questions for You to Answer, Plus a Podcast Example to Consider

Make sure you can answer these tech-related questions about your business:

- What tools do I need?
- How long will these tools be relevant?
- How will the information be used?

Let's consider our fitness instructor turned podcaster's answers to these questions.

What tools do you need?

For podcasting, the tools are fairly straightforward. You need to buy a few pieces of hardware and a lot of pay-as-you-go software. Notice this question says *need*! Focus on the needs only. A computer with a camera and a mic is likely enough to get started. Let the software do the rest of the work. There is no need for "a podcast mic" with today's technology and the resources you already have in hand. Our fitness trainer has an iPhone and AirPods. That equipment is used by big media every day, so that's good enough here, too.

How long will these tools be relevant?

If you focus on needs and hardware that has an overlapping purpose, like an iPhone, you will likely refresh the hardware regularly and stay current with the industry needs. If there are specialty items that pop up as you go, then consider them at that point. A fitness trainer can record audio and video on the phone for both live and recorded purposes. Perhaps a laptop supplements the more formal recording sessions and allows the phone to be an alternative camera or recording device.

When you need a specialty product, think long and hard about it. Technology moves fast and the trends move even faster. Our podcaster may want to buy a BMI measurement machine, but is it truly necessary? The tape measure and calipers are cheaper and are still relevant today!

How will the information be used?

Our podcaster may want to have a landing page where they can get subscribers pointed to a website for special events. Once someone registers for a special event, you have all of that contact info for future use (assuming you observe all privacy laws). Perhaps that is your marketing list when you launch your training video subscription. Maybe that is the same list you use for introducing your new hire.

In the same thought process, tracking individual fitness progress might be helpful for future advertising. Explaining how you have helped hundreds of clients lose thousands of pounds is different from saying, "My average client seeking to lose weight got to their target weight in an average of nine months." The details matter.

CHAPTER 15
RISK MANAGEMENT

In sports, teams must always be prepared for both the expected and the unexpected. The expected may be building a strategy around a star opponent. The unexpected, like injuries, weather conditions, or unexpected plays from the competition, can change the outcome of a game. Similarly, risks are inevitable in business. Whether it's financial uncertainty, changes in market conditions, legal challenges, or operational disruptions, every business faces risks. The key to success is not avoiding risks but managing them effectively.

Risk management is the process of identifying, assessing, and mitigating the potential threats that could harm your business. It's about developing strategies to minimize the impact of these risks and being prepared to respond when challenges arise. In this chapter, we will explore the importance of risk management, the types of risks your business might face, and strategies for building resilience and protecting your business from the unexpected.

Identifying Potential Risks: Understanding Your Business's Vulnerabilities

The first step in risk management is identifying the potential risks that could affect your business. Just as a coach assesses the opposing team's strengths and weaknesses before a game, you need to assess the vulnerabilities in your business. Risks come in many forms, and understanding where your business is most vulnerable will help you create a plan to address those risks.

FINANCIAL RISKS

One of the biggest risks businesses face is financial uncertainty. This can include cash flow issues, fluctuating market conditions, changes in customer demand, or unexpected expenses. Assess your financial stability and ensure you have sufficient cash reserves, a solid budgeting process, and contingency plans in place.

OPERATIONAL RISKS

Operational risks stem from issues that disrupt your day-to-day business activities. This can include supply chain disruptions, equipment failure, or employee turnover. Identify the critical operations in your business and assess the risks that could disrupt them. Consider contingency plans, backup suppliers, or cross-training employees to minimize the impact of operational risks.

REPUTATIONAL RISKS

Your brand's reputation is one of your most valuable assets, and reputational risks can cause long-term damage to your business. Negative publicity, poor customer service, or product failures can all impact how your business is perceived. Monitor customer feedback, address complaints promptly, and ensure that your business operates with integrity to protect your reputation.

LEGAL AND REGULATORY RISKS

Every business must comply with laws and regulations, and failing to do so can result in fines, lawsuits, or other penalties. This includes everything from tax laws to employment regulations and industry-specific standards. Regularly review your compliance obligations, and ensure that your business is up to date with any changes in the legal and regulatory landscape.

TECHNOLOGY AND CYBERSECURITY RISKS

In today's digital world, cybersecurity is a significant concern for businesses of all sizes. Data breaches, hacking attempts, and other cyber threats can result in financial losses and reputational damage. Invest in cybersecurity measures such as firewalls, encryption, and regular data backups to protect your business from cyber threats.

Assessing Risk: Evaluating the Likelihood and Impact

Not all risks are created equal — some may be highly likely to occur but have a minimal impact, while others may be less likely but have severe consequences. Just as a coach prioritizes game strategies based on the opponent's strengths and weaknesses, you need to prioritize risks based on their likelihood and potential impact.

1. How likely is the risk to occur? Some risks, such as changes in market conditions or supply chain disruptions, may be more likely to happen, while others, such as natural disasters, may be less frequent but still possible.
2. What would the consequences be if the risk occurred? Some risks, like minor equipment failures, may have a minimal impact on your business, while others, like a major data breach, could cause significant financial losses and damage your reputation.

A risk matrix is a useful tool for evaluating risks based on their likelihood and impact. Risks that are highly likely and have a high impact should be prioritized for mitigation, while those with low likelihood and low impact may require less attention.

Mitigating Risks: Developing a Risk Management Strategy

Once you've assessed your risks, the next step is developing strategies to mitigate them. There are several ways to mitigate risks:

- Avoidance: In some cases, the best way to manage a risk is to avoid it altogether. This might involve choosing not to engage in high-risk activities, or avoiding certain markets or products that carry significant risks.
- Reduction: Reducing risk involves taking steps to minimize the likelihood or impact of a risk. For example, you might invest in employee training to reduce the risk of accidents, or implement cybersecurity measures to reduce the risk of data breaches.
- Transfer: Transferring risk involves shifting the responsibility for managing the risk to another party. This can include purchasing insurance policies that cover certain types of risks, such as property damage, liability, or cyberattacks.
- Acceptance: Some risks cannot be avoided, reduced, or transferred. In these cases, you may choose to accept the risk and develop contingency plans to deal with it if it occurs. For example, a business might accept the risk of occasional equipment breakdowns and have a repair plan in place.

Creating a Risk Response Plan: Preparing for the Unexpected

Having a plan in place for how you will respond to risks when they occur is essential to minimizing their impact on your business. Just as a sports team practices specific plays to respond to different game situations, your business should have a risk response plan that outlines how you will react to various risks.

RESPONSE STRATEGIES

Develop specific strategies for responding to different types of risks. For example, how will you handle a supply chain disruption? What will you do if a major client defaults on a payment? Having predefined response strategies will allow you to act quickly and effectively when risks arise.

EMERGENCY COMMUNICATION

In the event of a significant risk such as a natural disaster or data breach, clear communication is essential. Ensure that your team knows who is responsible for communicating with employees, customers, suppliers, and other stakeholders. This will help you manage the situation more effectively and minimize confusion.

BUSINESS CONTINUITY PLAN

A business continuity plan outlines how your business will continue to operate in the event of a major disruption. This could include backup systems, alternative suppliers, or remote work arrangements. Having a business continuity plan in place ensures that your business can keep running in the face of significant challenges.

Monitoring and Reviewing Risks: Staying Proactive

Risk management is not a one-time effort—it's an ongoing process. Schedule regular reviews of your risk management plan to ensure that it remains up to date. This should include reviewing new risks, reassessing existing risks, and updating your mitigation strategies as needed.

It's also important to stay informed. The business environment is constantly changing, and new risks can emerge at any time. Stay informed about changes in your industry, market conditions, legal requirements, and technological developments that could impact your business.

Every time a risk occurs, use it as a learning opportunity. Review how well your risk management strategies worked, what could have been done differently, and how you can improve your response in the future.

Risk Management as a Strategic Advantage

All businesses have risk. However, it's important to realize that we all have a risk bias: Most of the time your perspective about the risk is the actual variable at play. The most frequent one I see professionally is familiarity bias. This is where people tend to prefer familiar options over unfamiliar ones. Thus, we may take on a known risk rather than an unknown risk. It is thus important to have outside perspective on the various risks of your business, business decisions, and strategies so you can proceed with the appropriate mitigation tactics in place.

Effective risk management is about more than just avoiding disasters — it's about building resilience and using risk as a strategic advantage. By identifying potential risks, assessing their likelihood and impact, and developing strategies to mitigate and respond to them, you can protect your business from harm and ensure its long-term success. With a strong risk management plan in place, your business will be well-positioned to navigate challenges and seize new opportunities as they arise.

Questions for You to Answer, Plus a Podcast Example to Consider

Prepare for risk by answering these questions:

- What is the biggest risk I might face?
- What is my tolerance for risk?
- How can I best leverage risk for the appropriate return?

Now, how might our fitness instructor turned podcaster answer these queries?

What is the biggest risk I might face?

Risks in podcasting are minimal. The first amendment right to free speech is fairly broad; however, spreading misinformation may directly impact your customer base. The biggest risk to our fitness trainer in the podcast is the financial commitment. The second would be the potential for reputational harm if the audience does not like or believe in the messages from the various episodes. However, once a client converts from listening to active participation in training, the risk of injury becomes the biggest concern.

What is my tolerance for risk?

Financial risk is part of being a small business owner. Honestly, business owners want the reward of the risk they face. One of the biggest factors of success for a podcast is longevity, so creating the resources in advance to give the podcast a long shelf life is important. Online research shows that 90 percent of podcasts don't go past episode three.[7] The podcaster may want to decide how much time (how many episodes) they're

---

[7] Samuel Sleger, "How to outlast 99% of podcasts: four simple rules," *Podnews*, May 28, 2025, https://podnews.net/article/four-rules-to-outlast-almost-every-other-podcast.

willing to commit to before expecting to see a return on that time investment.

How can I best leverage risk for the appropriate return?

This is the magic question. Obviously, you have to have an objective in mind to even get started, but I think it is important to remain malleable while sticking to the goal. Creating short, realistic goals about the podcast in the beginning are key. Remember, the focus is advertising and creating content for videos. You can quantify the videos and video hours, so focus there. That will give a sense of accomplishment.

Remaining flexible but focused is hard. However, you have to go where the client base needs are. Maybe your passion is discussing the intricacy of heavy lifting, but most of your clients don't do that. So don't spend your time there. Use analytics to pinpoint the messaging that hits the most people.

CHAPTER 16
CUSTOMER EXPERIENCE

In sports, fans are the lifeblood of any team. They provide support, loyalty, and excitement, and their experience during games, whether in the stadium or watching from home, plays a crucial role in their continued enthusiasm. In business, your customers are your "fans." Their experience with your brand can make or break your success. A great customer experience leads to loyal customers who advocate for your business, while a poor experience can lead to lost opportunities and reputational damage.

Customer experience (CX) encompasses every interaction a customer has with your business, from the moment they learn about your product or service to the support they receive after making a purchase. It's not just about making a sale — it's about creating a positive, memorable journey that encourages customers to come back and spread the word about your business.

In this chapter, we will explore how to create an exceptional customer experience, the key touchpoints to focus on, and how to turn satisfied customers into loyal advocates.

Understanding the Customer Journey: Mapping Every Touchpoint

The customer experience is not limited to one moment in time — it's a journey that spans multiple touchpoints. Understanding the customer journey is essential to delivering a seamless, enjoyable experience at every stage. The stages include:

AWARENESS

The customer journey begins when a potential customer first becomes aware of your business. This could be through advertising, social media, word-of-mouth, or search engine results. At this stage, it's crucial to make a positive first impression and ensure that your messaging is clear, compelling, and aligned with your brand values.

CONSIDERATION

Once a customer is aware of your business, they will begin evaluating whether your product or service meets their needs. This is where your website, product descriptions, reviews, and customer service come into play. Providing clear information, addressing potential concerns, and offering valuable content can help move the customer from consideration to decision.

PURCHASE

The purchase stage is a critical touchpoint in the customer journey. A seamless, user-friendly checkout process can make the difference between a completed sale and an abandoned cart. Whether your customers are purchasing online or in store, ensure that the process is intuitive, secure, and as simple as possible.

POST PURCHASE

The customer experience doesn't end when a purchase is made. In fact, it's just the beginning of the relationship. Providing excellent post-purchase support, whether through clear communication, easy returns, or helpful customer service, ensures that customers feel valued and satisfied. This is the stage where you can turn one-time buyers into loyal customers.

LOYALTY AND ADVOCACY

The final stage of the customer journey is loyalty and advocacy. When customers have a positive experience, they are more likely to return for future purchases and recommend your business to others. Encourage repeat business through loyalty programs, personalized offers, and ongoing engagement.

Creating a Customer-Centric Culture

At the heart of a great customer experience is a customer-centric culture — an organizational mindset that puts the customer's needs and satisfaction at the forefront of everything you do. Just as a sports team is dedicated to giving fans a great game day experience, your business should be focused on delivering exceptional service at every customer touchpoint. To do this, you can:

- Empower employees. When employees feel valued and supported, they are more likely to deliver excellent service. Empower your employees to go above and beyond for customers by providing them with the tools, training, and autonomy they need to solve problems and create positive interactions.
- Listen to customers. Whether through surveys, reviews, or direct communication, seek out feedback to understand what customers love about your business and where improvements are needed. Show customers that their opinions matter by implementing changes based on their feedback.
- Provide consistency across touchpoints. Customers should have a consistent experience, whether they interact with your business online, over the phone, or in person. Ensure that your messaging, tone, and level of service are consistent, no matter where or how customers engage with your business.

- Personalize. In today's digital world, customers expect personalized experiences. Use data to tailor your communications to each customer's preferences. Personalized recommendations, targeted marketing, and customized support make customers feel valued and understood, leading to stronger relationships and increased loyalty.

Exceeding Customer Expectations: Going the Extra Mile

To stand out in a competitive marketplace, it's not enough to meet customer expectations—you need to exceed them. What's the difference between meeting versus exceeding expectations? These behaviors are the key.

BE PROACTIVE

Anticipate your customers' needs and address potential issues before they arise. For example, if a product is out of stock, offer alternative suggestions or provide updates on when it will be available. Proactively reaching out to customers when you foresee an issue shows that you're attentive and committed to their satisfaction.

OFFER VALUE-ADDED SERVICES

Adding extra value to your products or services can set your business apart. This could include offering free shipping, extended warranties, or complimentary support. Value-added services enhance the customer experience and give customers more reasons to choose your business over competitors.

SURPRISE AND DELIGHT

Small, unexpected gestures can go a long way in building customer loyalty. This might involve sending a personalized thank-you note, offering a surprise discount, or including a small gift with a purchase. These thoughtful touches show customers that you appreciate their business and are willing to go the extra mile to make them feel special.

SOLVE PROBLEMS QUICKLY AND EFFECTIVELY

No matter how great your product or service is, problems will inevitably arise. What matters most is how you handle them. When customers encounter an issue, respond promptly and work to resolve it as quickly and efficiently as possible. A well-handled problem can turn a negative experience into a positive one, reinforcing the customer's trust in your brand.

Measuring and Improving Customer Experience

To continually improve the customer experience, it's essential to measure how well you're doing and identify areas for improvement. Key CX metrics include:

- Customer Satisfaction (CSAT): CSAT surveys measure how satisfied customers are with your product, service, or overall experience. Use CSAT surveys after key touchpoints, such as after a purchase, to gauge satisfaction and identify areas for improvement.
- Net Promoter Score (NPS): NPS measures customer loyalty by asking how likely customers are to recommend your business to others. A high NPS indicates that customers are happy with their experience and are likely to become brand advocates, while a low NPS suggests that there may be issues to address.
- Customer Effort Score (CES): CES measures how easy it is for customers to interact with your business. Whether it's making a purchase, getting support, or finding information, reducing customer effort is key to providing a seamless

experience. Use CES to identify friction points in the customer journey and make improvements.

In addition to formal metrics, qualitative customer feedback provides valuable insights into their experience. Regularly go through customer reviews, comments, and social media mentions to understand what's working well and where there's room for improvement.

Turning Customers into Advocates

A great customer experience doesn't just lead to satisfied customers — it creates loyal advocates who spread the word about your business. Customer advocacy is one of the most powerful forms of marketing, as people are more likely to trust recommendations from friends and family over traditional advertising. Here's how you can facilitate it:

ENCOURAGE REVIEWS AND TESTIMONIALS

Happy customers are often willing to share their positive experiences — sometimes they just need a little nudge. Encourage satisfied customers to leave reviews, provide testimonials, or share their experiences on social media. Positive reviews help build trust with potential customers and showcase your commitment to excellence.

CREATE REFERRAL PROGRAMS

Incentivize your customers to refer their friends and family by offering rewards, such as discounts, free products, or exclusive offers. Referral programs not only bring in new customers but also strengthen the relationship with existing ones by showing that you value their support.

BUILD A COMMUNITY

Create opportunities for customers to engage with your brand and each other through events, social media groups, or exclusive online forums. Building a community around your brand fosters loyalty and gives customers a sense of belonging, turning them into passionate advocates for your business.

A Tactical Approach to Creating Unforgettable Customer Experiences

Most of the time you know a lot of these elements in your head, and they are built into other tasks that you perform. I fully recognize something like this may seem very far-fetched for a new business owner. However, a lot of the experience elements outlined here can be thought about in the form of a Google or Yelp review. Ultimately, your focus is to make sure that the client got what they wanted out of the situation to maximize the opportunity for repeat business.

Customer experience is about more than just providing a good product or service — it's about creating memorable, positive interactions that keep customers coming back. By understanding the customer journey, fostering a customer-centric culture, exceeding expectations, and continuously measuring and improving your efforts, you can build a loyal customer base that drives your business's success.

Remember, happy customers are not just repeat buyers — they are your biggest advocates, spreading the word and helping your business grow. By prioritizing customer experience, you can turn everyday customers into lifelong fans who are excited to support your brand.

Questions for You to Answer, Plus a Podcast Example to Consider

Here are essential customer experience considerations to keep in mind:

- What's the anticipated roadmap for the CX?
- What did I find to be an obstruction I didn't anticipate?
- How can I get this information to act upon?

How might our fitness instructor turned podcaster answer these questions? Let's see.

What's the anticipated roadmap for the CX?

Think of this as a storyboard-type scenario. If our fitness instructor broke things down into phases it would look something like this:

- Discovery: A potential listener will be judging the title, graphics, and synopsis of the podcast. Will they opt in and listen?
- First engagement: Once the listener hits play, every detail matters. The sound quality, the host's voice and delivery, the story, the flow, and the overall vibe all matter in portraying something to the listener. In the end, if it sounds right and feels authentic, you have the opportunity to connect. The key question is: was the message relatable and compelling enough to make them want more?
- Interaction and follow-up: If the listener likes what they hear, they will be looking for ways to engage further. What resources are available to keep them engaged?
- Community and loyalty building: A listener may want more than just the podcast. How can the listener learn more about you and the various guests? Are you active on

social sites to help supplement engagement in between episodes?
- Long-term value and monetization: A potential listener may listen a few times or even multiple episodes before taking action. Do you have calls to action to hit the intended result of getting hired or selling your subscription program?

What did you find to be an obstruction you didn't anticipate?

This is where a crystal ball might be helpful. Perhaps you have a guest on the show and that guest ends up taking some of what you hoped your customer base might have been. Whoops! You will have to stay nimble to make sure you adjust your message along the way to hit the goals.

How can you get this information to act upon?

Sometimes you can't know this information until after the fact. Sometimes you get it on the fly. There is no perfect way to get customer feedback and adapt. What's important is that you do it. Paying attention to comments on the show pages, seeking feedback from listeners via email or text, and even asking friends and family for feedback is helpful. Just remember to react and reflect. Do not overreact.

Sometimes what is a good customer experience for one person is a terrible one for another. Many factors can trigger that negative customer, but let's assume you made no mistakes. Sometimes the CX just isn't for that person. You have one of two decisions: Dig deeper and see if you can adjust to accommodate more people like that consumer, or focus more on the types of customers who had a positive experience. Both are viable decisions.

CHAPTER 17
NETWORKING AND PARTNERSHIPS

In sports, success often relies not just on the players on the field but also on the support and collaboration of others like coaches, trainers, sponsors, and partners. The same is true in business. Building strong relationships through networking and forming strategic partnerships can open new doors, create opportunities, and help you grow your business faster than you could on your own.

Networking allows you to connect with other professionals, exchange ideas, gain valuable insights, and discover potential collaborations. Partnerships, on the other hand, are formalized relationships in which you and another business or individual work together to achieve mutual goals. Both are essential for expanding your business's reach, gaining access to new resources, and staying competitive in your industry.

In this chapter, we will explore how to build effective networks, cultivate meaningful partnerships, and leverage these relationships to drive growth and success for your business.

The Importance of Networking: Building Meaningful Connections

Networking is about building relationships with people who can support and contribute to your business goals. The more people you know, the more opportunities you'll have. Attend industry events, join professional organizations, and participate in online forums or social media groups relevant to your industry. These platforms provide a wealth of opportunities to meet new people, learn from others, and grow your professional network.

With that said, networking isn't just about collecting business cards or connecting on LinkedIn — it's about building genuine relationships. Take the time to get to know the people in your network. Understand their needs, challenges, and goals, and offer your support where possible. Building trust and rapport is the foundation of any strong network.

Also, recognize that networking is a two-way street. Share your knowledge, offer assistance, and look for ways to help others in your network. In doing so, you'll build stronger, more meaningful connections that can benefit both parties in the long run.

Finally, realize that a strong network requires ongoing effort. Regularly engage with the people in your network — whether through social media, email, or face-to-face meetings. Staying in touch ensures that you remain top of mind and that you're continually building and strengthening your relationships.

Leveraging Your Network for Business Growth

Once you've built a solid network, it's time to leverage those relationships to grow your business. Your network can provide valuable resources, insights, and opportunities that might not be available otherwise.

GAINING NEW CLIENTS AND CUSTOMERS

One of the most direct benefits of networking is the potential to gain new clients or customers. Referrals from trusted contacts in your network can lead to new business opportunities. When someone in your network recommends your services, it adds credibility and trust, making it more likely that potential clients will choose to work with you.

LEARNING FROM OTHERS

Networking gives you access to a wealth of knowledge and experience. Whether it's advice on solving a business problem, insights into market trends, or recommendations for service providers, your network can serve as a valuable resource for learning and growing. Don't hesitate to seek out mentors, ask questions, and learn from those who have more experience.

FINDING COLLABORATORS

Your network is also a great place to find potential collaborators. Whether it's working together on a project, co-hosting an event, or sharing resources, collaborating with others in your network can lead to mutually beneficial opportunities. Collaboration allows you to combine strengths and expand your reach in ways that wouldn't be possible alone.

STAYING INFORMED

In business, staying up to date with industry trends and changes is crucial. Your network can help you stay informed about what's happening in your industry — whether it's new technology, regulatory changes, or emerging opportunities. Being in the loop ensures that you can adapt and make informed decisions for your business.

Building Strategic Partnerships: Collaboration for Mutual Success

While networking helps you build connections, strategic partnerships take those relationships a step further. We discussed strategic partnerships earlier in Chapter 4, so you can reference the specifics there; however, it's important to realize that strategic partnerships can help accelerate success and growth.

IDENTIFYING POTENTIAL PARTNERS

Start by identifying businesses or individuals that share your goals, target audience, or values. Look for partners whose strengths complement yours. For example, if you're a service-based business, you might partner with a product-based business that serves the same market, allowing you to offer a more comprehensive solution to customers.

ESTABLISHING CLEAR GOALS

Before entering into a partnership, it's important to define the goals and objectives of the collaboration. What do both parties hope to achieve? Whether it's increasing market share, reaching new customers, or sharing expertise, having clear goals ensures that both parties are aligned and working toward mutual success.

CREATING WIN-WIN AGREEMENTS

Successful partnerships are built on mutual benefit. Both parties should feel that they are gaining value from the collaboration. Clearly outline the roles, responsibilities, and expectations for each partner, and ensure that both parties contribute fairly to the partnership.

MAINTAINING STRONG COMMUNICATION

Like any relationship, communication is key to a successful partnership. Regularly check in with your partners to ensure that the collaboration is progressing as planned and that both parties are satisfied with the arrangement. Open communication helps resolve any issues that arise and keeps the partnership on track.

NURTURING MUTUAL RESPECT AND TRUST

Successful partnerships are built on trust and respect. Ensure that both parties fulfill their obligations and respect each other's contributions to the partnership. Trust is key to maintaining a positive and long-lasting relationship.

ADAPTING TO CHANGE

Business environments are constantly changing, and partnerships need to adapt to remain relevant. Be open to adjusting the terms of the partnership as needed to reflect new opportunities, challenges, or market conditions. Flexibility is essential for maintaining a successful partnership in the long term.

CELEBRATING SUCCESSES

Take the time to celebrate the successes that result from your partnership. Whether it's reaching a sales milestone, launching a new product, or achieving a mutual goal, acknowledging and celebrating successes strengthens the relationship and sets the stage for future collaboration.

Types of Business Partnerships

There are many different types of business partnerships, each with its own benefits and challenges. Understanding the different types of partnerships can help you choose the best approach for your business.

- Joint ventures: A joint venture is a formal agreement between two or more businesses to work together on a specific project or initiative. Joint ventures are often used for short-term collaborations, such as launching a new product or entering a new market. The businesses involved share both the risks and the rewards.
- Strategic alliances: Strategic alliances are less formal than joint ventures but still involve collaboration between two or more businesses. In a strategic alliance, businesses work together to achieve common goals, such as sharing market insights, co-marketing, or developing new products. Unlike joint ventures, each business remains independent.

- Supplier partnerships: Partnering with your suppliers can help strengthen your supply chain and ensure that you receive high-quality materials or products. These partnerships often involve long-term agreements, bulk discounts, or exclusive arrangements that benefit both parties.
- Referral partnerships: Referral partnerships involve businesses agreeing to refer clients or customers to one another. This type of partnership is especially useful for businesses that offer complementary services. For example, a web design company might refer clients to a digital marketing agency, and vice versa.

The Key to Networking? Just Start Somewhere

Without networking experience or scenarios where you have developed these types of relationships before, it can be hard to fully grasp how to do it. So often we are pressed for time and many times certain folks are very focused on the transactional elements of a relationship. When I attend networking events, I am inevitably approached by people who want to do business with me because I am either a good target for their goods or services, or I am perceived to have a client base that is a good target. A few will try to do the hard sell to get an immediate deal. Unless I show up with a specific need in mind, this is not my style — and I am not afraid to tell folks that. Sometimes this is off-putting, but it helps clear out space for the relational elements.

Timing is everything here. If you need it now and give it no forethought, you'll take who is available and possibly sacrifice quality to get the result. However, if you develop your list of resources, you will generally have the right fit available for your needs. Instead of feeling the need to hard sell someone upon a first meeting at a networking event, you will have a roster of contacts at your fingertips.

In business, just like in sports, success often depends on the strength of the team, both on and off the field. Networking and partnerships allow you to expand your business's reach, gain access to new resources, and collaborate with others to achieve mutual success. By building a strong network, forming strategic partnerships, and maintaining those relationships over time, you can create a powerful support system that drives growth and helps your business thrive.

Questions for You to Answer, Plus a Podcast Example to Consider

Ask yourself these questions to gauge your network:

- Do I have a professional network?
- Who would I want as strategic partners?
- Have I leveraged my network for my benefit before?

Now let's put those questions to our fitness instructor turned podcaster.

Do you have a professional network?

Those new to an industry may not have a formal network. Finding one is key. Our podcaster knows no one in the media industry and has little experience using this type of information for their benefit. The game plan is to rely on the podcast producer and the folks that the production company might work with. Although this might not immediately yield results, it will yield contacts. Utilize those contacts and remember: just start somewhere!

Who would you want as strategic partners?

As a fitness trainer and podcaster, five strategic partnerships that might be of immediate relevance: gyms and gym owners;

athletic leagues and schools; community health and wellness centers; podcast networks and producers; and podcast guests.

Have you leveraged your network for your benefit before?

A lot of people have never had to do this and do not know how. Neither does our fitness trainer! There is certainly an art to this and those who do it well are true masters at their craft. If our podcaster wanted to improve her networking skills, she might join a networking group or follow experienced members to learn from their approach.

For those who have done this, remember that in the beginning, the power of an ask can go a really long way. Asking a new contact to listen to your podcast and explaining how that could really help your business costs you nothing. At best, you get this person's training business. At worst, you asked!

CHAPTER 18
ADAPTABILITY AND INNOVATION

In sports, teams that fail to adapt to new strategies, changing player dynamics, or evolving competition often fall behind. The same is true in business. Adaptability and innovation are critical to staying competitive in an ever-changing market. Businesses that can pivot, embrace new technologies, and find creative solutions to challenges not only survive but thrive.

Adaptability is the ability to adjust to changing circumstances, whether they are internal or external. Innovation is the process of creating new ideas, products, services, or processes that bring value to your business and customers. Together, these qualities allow businesses to stay ahead of the curve and remain resilient in the face of challenges.

In this chapter, we will explore why adaptability and innovation are essential for long-term business success. We will discuss how to foster a culture of innovation, including using strategies for staying agile in a rapidly changing world.

The Importance of Adaptability: Thriving in a Changing Environment

Adaptability is more than just reacting to change — it's about anticipating and preparing for it. In a fast-paced world, market conditions, customer preferences, and technological advancements can shift rapidly, and businesses must be able to respond effectively. Remaining adaptive requires the following:

- Anticipating change: While you can't predict the future, you can stay informed about trends and changes that might impact your business. Whether it's advancements in technology, shifts in customer behavior, or changes in regulations, being aware of the factors that could affect your industry allows you to prepare and respond more effectively.
- Agility in decision making: Agile decision making is key to adaptability. In a rapidly changing environment, waiting too long to make decisions can result in missed opportunities. Train your team to make quick, informed decisions based on available data, and empower them to act without unnecessary delays.
- Embracing flexibility: Flexibility is at the heart of adaptability. Whether it's adjusting your business model, reallocating resources, or changing your approach to problem-solving, being flexible allows your business to respond to challenges and seize opportunities as they arise.
- Building resilience: Adaptability is closely tied to resilience — the ability to recover quickly from setbacks. Businesses that can bounce back from failure, learn from their mistakes, and continue moving forward are more likely to succeed in the long run. Encourage a culture that views challenges as learning opportunities rather than insurmountable obstacles.

Fostering a Culture of Innovation: Encouraging Creative Thinking

Innovation is essential for staying competitive and driving growth. Businesses that innovate are able to introduce new products, services, or processes that add value for customers and set them apart from competitors.

ENCOURAGING EXPERIMENTATION

Innovation requires a willingness to experiment and take risks. Encourage your team to think creatively, explore new ideas, and experiment with different approaches. Not every idea will be a success, but fostering an environment where employees feel safe to innovate without fear of failure is key to discovering groundbreaking solutions.

COLLABORATION ACROSS DEPARTMENTS

Innovation often happens at the intersection of different perspectives. Encourage collaboration across departments and disciplines to generate new ideas and solutions. Just as a sports team thrives when players work together, your business can benefit from diverse viewpoints working in harmony to drive innovation.

RECOGNIZING AND REWARDING INNOVATION

Celebrate innovative ideas, even if they don't always lead to immediate success. Recognizing and rewarding employees for their creativity encourages them to continue thinking outside the box. This recognition can come in the form of public acknowledgment, bonuses, or opportunities to lead new initiatives.

INVESTING IN RESEARCH AND DEVELOPMENT (R&D)

Innovation doesn't happen by accident—it requires resources. Investing in R&D allows your business to explore new technologies, test new products, and develop innovative solutions that give you a competitive edge. Whether it's investing in new software, tools, or expertise, R&D is essential for continuous innovation.

Leveraging Technology for Innovation and Adaptability

Technology plays a critical role in both adaptability and innovation. Just as sports teams use data analytics, advanced training tools, and communication technology to improve performance, businesses can leverage technology to drive innovation and stay agile.

ADOPTING NEW TECHNOLOGIES

Stay up to date with technological advancements in your industry and be willing to adopt new tools and platforms that can improve efficiency, productivity, and customer satisfaction. Whether it's implementing automation to streamline operations or using AI to enhance customer service, adopting the right technology can keep your business competitive.

DATA-DRIVEN DECISION MAKING

Data analytics is a powerful tool for both innovation and adaptability. By analyzing data on customer behavior, market trends, and operational performance, you can make informed decisions that help you innovate and respond to change more effectively. Data-driven insights can lead to the development of new products, services, and strategies that are tailored to customer needs.

CLOUD-BASED SOLUTIONS

Cloud-based technology offers flexibility and scalability, allowing your business to adapt quickly to changing conditions. With cloud-based systems, your team can access critical data and tools from anywhere, enabling remote work, collaboration, and seamless communication. Cloud solutions also make it easier to scale your operations as your business grows.

STAYING AGILE IN PRODUCT DEVELOPMENT

Agile methodologies are widely used in technology development, but they can also be applied to other areas of your business. By using iterative processes, rapid prototyping, and feedback loops, you can develop new products and services more quickly and efficiently. This approach allows you to test and refine ideas in real-time, ensuring that you're meeting customer needs and staying ahead of competitors.

Overcoming Barriers to Innovation

While innovation is essential, it's not without its challenges. Many businesses face barriers that prevent them from fully embracing innovation, whether it's fear of failure, resistance to change, or resource constraints. Overcoming these barriers is key to unlocking your business's potential for growth.

OVERCOMING RESISTANCE TO CHANGE

Change can be difficult, especially for businesses that have been doing things the same way for years. To overcome resistance, communicate the benefits of innovation and adaptability to your team. Help employees understand why change is necessary and how it will benefit both the business and their individual roles.

MANAGING RISK

Innovation often involves taking risks, but that doesn't mean being reckless. Manage risk by testing new ideas on a small scale before fully committing to them. Pilot programs, MVPs (minimum viable products), and incremental improvements allow you to experiment with new ideas while minimizing the potential downsides.

ALLOCATING RESOURCES

Innovation requires time, money, and effort. Ensure that you're allocating sufficient resources to support innovation initiatives, whether it's investing in new technology, hiring additional talent, or providing training and development. Without the right resources, even the best ideas might never come to fruition.

BREAKING DOWN SILOS

Organizational silos can stifle innovation by preventing collaboration and information sharing. Encourage cross-departmental collaboration and communication to break down these barriers and foster a more open, innovative culture. Just as sports teams rely on every player working together, your business needs all departments to collaborate for successful innovation.

Adapting to Market Changes and Customer Needs

In business, customer needs and market conditions are constantly evolving. Staying adaptable and innovative ensures that your business remains relevant and continues to meet the changing demands of your customers. You can do that by:

- Listening to customers. Regularly engage with your customers to understand their pain points, desires, and expectations. Through surveys, focus groups, or direct communication, customer insights can inspire new products, services, or improvements to existing offerings.
- Tracking industry trends. Attend industry conferences, subscribe to trade publications, and follow thought leaders in your field to stay informed about the latest developments. Being aware of trends allows you to anticipate changes and position your business for success.
- Pivoting when necessary. Sometimes, market conditions or customer needs change so dramatically that your business needs to pivot. Whether it's adjusting your product line, changing your marketing strategy, or entering a new

market, being able to pivot quickly ensures that your business remains relevant and competitive.

Adaptability and Innovation as Keys to Long-Term Success

In sports and business, there needs to be a level of predictability and repetitiveness that allows you to achieve certain objectives. From season to season, there may be small rule changes that adjust your tactics during the game, but those changes do not fundamentally change how the game is played. Soccer rule changes did not magically allow everyone to use their hands. From this standpoint the fundamentals of the game have remained the same since the beginning.

In business, however, the rules may change entirely — they might suddenly allow you to use your hands. During the COVID pandemic, restaurants were not allowed to host guests, so many adapted to accommodate takeout orders where previously they did not. Some chose not to do so because they were not able to maintain the same food quality standards and therefore adapted in other ways.

In business, things will change. If you cannot accept that now, do not be a business owner. The key is figuring out how to weave adaptability into your day-to-day behavior and business culture so that when change is needed, the change is not an excuse or reason to miss the mark. You just figure it out.

I teach this to my soccer players in one specific way every season: I repetitively make "bad calls" in practice. One constant in sports is that a call by an official may be perceived as a bad call. I have found that it is very, very rare that a referee decides the game by making a bad call. That is just the excuse people focus on. So, we weave that into the expectation at practice because I know it will happen in a game. I want my players to perform regardless of a good or a bad call.

Just to be clear, my bad calls in practice are egregious. For example, I randomly red card players or award penalties on the wrong end of the field for no foul at all. In the beginning, no one understands what is happening. Over time, we laugh about it. The lesson: You must embrace the predictable and unpredictable, and make the unpredictable as predictable as possible.

In business, as in sports, the ability to adapt and innovate is critical to long-term success. Markets change, customer preferences shift, and new competitors emerge — staying ahead of the curve requires a commitment to continuous improvement and a willingness to embrace change.

By fostering a culture of innovation, leveraging technology, and staying flexible in the face of challenges, your business can not only survive but thrive in an ever-changing environment. Adaptability and innovation are not just about responding to change — they are about driving change and shaping the future of your business.

Questions for You to Answer, Plus a Podcast Example to Consider

Think about these questions for your own business:

- Where do I think I will need to be flexible to ensure success?
- Is it information, technology, equipment, or people that will require the most investment when change happens?
- How will I know when there is a change to consider or implement?

How might our fitness instructor turned podcaster answer these queries?

Where do you think you will need to be flexible to ensure success?

Podcasting is about creating both timely/relevant and evergreen content. Our fitness trainer will need to develop content that fits both spaces. Some needs to be regular, repeatable routines for folks to follow and use on demand. Some needs to be focused on new, relevant, and engaging topics to prove relevance and expertise in the industry *and* attract new customers.

Is it information, technology, equipment, or people that will require the most investment when change happens?

All four of these categories are relevant. Given the focus is to create content, information is highly likely to be the biggest need. Technology and equipment can likely be paired together, because much of the production and distribution process will be bundled with hardware and software that achieves the goal. Utilizing brand name hardware and software as a service type software might cost a little more but can ensure that you have what you need of current podcast recording technology. While people may not be the first thing that comes to mind in podcasting, they play a critical role. You'll have a host, guests, and a production person or team. If you lose the production person, will the new one know what target results to produce?

How will you know when there is a change to consider or implement?

Fitness trainers generally attend classes, work with others in the industry, and perform research. Let's call this continuing education and professional association networking. These groups will not only help in identifying industry trends but also in building an infrastructure. Separately, pulling information from actual client results, working with medical professionals, and studying outside factors can all lead to topic changes, format changes, or even changes in how frequently the podcast is produced and distributed.

CHAPTER 19
SUSTAINABILITY AND SOCIAL RESPONSIBILITY

In sports, many teams have a commitment that goes beyond the game. They aim to make a positive impact on their communities and the environment. Many may recall the story of Knute Rockne's "Win just one for the Gipper" in Notre Dame football.

The 1928 football season was one of the worst in Notre Dame history. At halftime of the Notre Dame v. Army contest, Coach Rockne told the story of George Gipp. Gipp was a star halfback who passed away in 1920. The abbreviated story is that Gipp asked Coach Rockne to have the team "Win one for the Gipper" someday. When Coach Rockne told that to the team, it created the extra motivation they needed to come out as the underdog winner.

The same mindset is becoming increasingly important in business. Today's consumers, employees, and investors are looking for companies that not only deliver great products and services but also operate with a sense of purpose, responsibility, and sustainability. Sustainability and social responsibility involve actively contributing to the well-being of society and the environment. Companies that embrace these principles gain the trust and loyalty of customers, build stronger relationships with stakeholders, and create long-term value that extends beyond profit margins.

In this chapter, we will explore how to integrate sustainability and social responsibility into your business strategy, the benefits of doing so, and the steps you can take to make a meaningful impact.

The Business Case for Sustainability: Long-Term Value Creation

Sustainability isn't just about protecting the planet — it's also about creating long-term business value. By reducing waste, conserving resources, and making ethical decisions, businesses can save money, improve efficiency, and strengthen their brand reputation.

REDUCING COSTS AND IMPROVING EFFICIENCY

Sustainable practices often lead to cost savings by reducing energy consumption, waste, and resource use. For example, switching to energy-efficient lighting, optimizing supply chain logistics, or reducing packaging materials can lower operational costs while benefiting the environment.

ENHANCING BRAND REPUTATION

Consumers today are more conscious of the ethical and environmental practices of the companies they support. Businesses that prioritize sustainability are more likely to attract and retain customers who value corporate responsibility. Just as sports teams build loyal fan bases through positive community involvement, businesses can strengthen customer loyalty by showing a commitment to sustainability.

ATTRACTING AND RETAINING TALENT

Employees, especially younger generations, are increasingly looking for employers that align with their values. By creating a workplace culture that prioritizes sustainability and social responsibility, you can attract top talent and boost employee satisfaction and retention.

MITIGATING RISK

Environmental and social risks, such as climate change or human rights violations, can have serious consequences for businesses.

By adopting sustainable practices, companies can reduce their exposure to these risks and ensure long-term stability.

Environmental Sustainability: Reducing Your Business's Footprint

Environmental sustainability involves minimizing the negative impact your business has on the planet. Just as athletes focus on maintaining their health and longevity through training and diet, businesses need to focus on reducing their environmental footprint to ensure a sustainable future. Here are key areas to focus on:

- Energy efficiency: Reducing energy consumption can include using energy-efficient lighting and equipment, optimizing heating and cooling systems, and incorporating renewable energy sources like solar or wind power into your operations.
- Waste reduction: Implement practices such as recycling, composting, and reusing materials where possible. In manufacturing, consider adopting a circular economy approach, where products are designed to be reused or recycled at the end of their lifecycle.
- Sustainable sourcing: Work with suppliers that prioritize sustainable practices, such as using renewable resources, reducing emissions, and ensuring fair labor practices. Sustainable sourcing ensures that your supply chain aligns with your environmental goals.
- Water conservation: Implement water-saving technologies in your operations, such as low-flow fixtures and rainwater harvesting systems. Additionally, consider the water footprint of your products and services and find ways to reduce consumption.

Social Responsibility: Making a Positive Impact on Society

Social responsibility is about contributing to the well-being of the communities where you operate. Businesses have a role to play in improving the lives of employees, customers, and society at large.

ETHICAL LABOR PRACTICES

Ensuring fair labor practices is a cornerstone of social responsibility. This means providing fair wages, safe working conditions, and equal opportunities for all employees. It also involves ensuring that your supply chain partners adhere to ethical labor standards, preventing practices like child labor or exploitation.

COMMUNITY ENGAGEMENT

Giving back to the community is a powerful way to build positive relationships and make a meaningful impact. This could involve sponsoring local events, supporting charitable causes, or encouraging employees to volunteer. Community engagement not only benefits those in need but also strengthens your brand's presence and goodwill.

DIVERSITY AND INCLUSION

Promoting diversity and inclusion within your organization is essential for social responsibility. A diverse workforce brings different perspectives, ideas, and experiences to the table, fostering innovation and creativity. Additionally, businesses that prioritize diversity and inclusion are more likely to build strong, inclusive communities both inside and outside the organization.

SUPPORTING HEALTH AND WELL-BEING

Whether it's providing health benefits for employees, promoting work-life balance, or supporting mental health initiatives, businesses have a responsibility to promote the well-being of their workforce. Investing in employee health and well-being not only improves productivity but also enhances employee satisfaction and loyalty.

Sustainable Innovation: Driving Positive Change

Innovation plays a crucial role in driving sustainability and social responsibility. Sustainable innovation allows businesses to meet the needs of today while ensuring that future generations can thrive.

DEVELOPING ECO-FRIENDLY PRODUCTS

One way to contribute to environmental sustainability is by developing products that have a lower environmental impact. This could include using sustainable materials, designing products that last longer, or creating items that can be easily recycled or composted at the end of their lifecycle.

SUSTAINABLE PACKAGING

Packaging is a significant contributor to waste, especially in industries like retail and e-commerce. Innovating in packaging design — by using biodegradable, reusable, or minimal packaging — can reduce your environmental footprint and appeal to environmentally conscious consumers.

DIGITAL TRANSFORMATION

Going digital can also contribute to sustainability. For example, replacing paper-based processes with digital systems can significantly reduce waste. Additionally, leveraging cloud technology for data storage and communication can reduce the need for physical infrastructure, cutting energy consumption and carbon emissions.

CREATING SHARED VALUE

Shared value is a business strategy that aligns social and environmental goals with economic success. By creating products or services that solve social or environmental problems, businesses can create new revenue streams while making a positive impact. For example, a company might develop a clean energy solution that both generates profits and helps reduce carbon emissions.

Measuring and Reporting Sustainability Efforts

Measuring the impact of your sustainability and social responsibility efforts is essential for accountability and continuous improvement. There are a number of tools for measuring and communicating these efforts.

Many businesses publish sustainability reports that outline their environmental and social performance. These reports often include metrics on energy consumption, waste reduction, emissions, and community impact. Publishing a sustainability report not only demonstrates transparency but also helps you track progress toward your sustainability goals.

Environmental, Social, and Governance (ESG) metrics are a standard way to measure a company's sustainability and social responsibility. These metrics cover a range of factors, including environmental impact, labor practices, and corporate governance. Many investors now consider ESG performance when making investment decisions, making it important for businesses to track and report these metrics.

Sustainability and social responsibility are ongoing efforts. Regularly reviewing your progress and identifying areas for improvement ensures that your business continues to evolve and make a positive impact. Set clear, measurable goals for your sustainability efforts and adjust your strategies as needed to meet those targets.

A Balanced Approach: Building a Sustainable and Responsible Business

Woven into this chapter are conversations about emotions, perhaps lifestyle choices, and other potentially charged topics. My goal is not to persuade anyone in one direction or another. It is simply to illustrate that all these variables are real-life factors.

In business, the choices you make will have an impact beyond your immediate bubble of influence. Without exception, our client list contains people that are seeking something beyond themselves. That is not to say that I do not have driven, successful, or perhaps greedy clients. What I can say is that there is always a larger motivation backed by some more significant mission. Maybe it is as simple as, "Give my kids a better life." Maybe it is providing gifts to community organizations, schools, or churches. What matters is recognizing that there is something beyond the business. Incorporating that into your business model will aid in the success of the business.

Sustainability and social responsibility are not just buzzwords — they are essential components of building a business that creates long-term value for customers, employees, and society. Just as sports teams succeed when they focus on more than just winning, businesses thrive when they operate with a broader sense of purpose.

By integrating sustainable practices into your operations, contributing to the well-being of your community, and innovating for positive change, you can build a business that not only performs well financially but also makes a lasting, positive impact on the world.

Questions for You to Answer, Plus a Podcast Example to Consider

Take a moment to reflect on your business purpose and then answer these questions:

- Do I have a cause beyond my business purpose and profit motive? If so, what is it?
- How does this cause offer a value proposition for both me and the consumer?
- Do I have a value proposition for my team that allows them to have something different than they would as part of my competitor's organization?
- Look back to the mission, vision, value statement created in Chapter 10. Does it require any adjustments?

Imagine our fitness trainer's philosophy is influenced by Peloton and consider the first question: If that were the case, would you have a cause beyond your business purpose and profit motive? If so, what is it?

If you are not familiar with Peloton's classes, they openly embrace all skill levels and all fitness commitments. Even in a workout, they offer alternatives for higher or lower levels. For our fitness trainer, the mission is to help people engage in a healthy lifestyle, no matter what. If someone goes for a walk during the podcast instead of sitting, the goal has been achieved: encouraging positive fitness changes for as many people as possible.

How does this cause offer a value proposition for both you and your consumer?

Reaching more people benefits the trainer because it may mean more clients. It benefits the consumer by creating accessible ways to improve fitness. The trainer can't do the work for the client, but they can help clear obstacles whether they are physical, mental, or time-related. Giving relatable examples is a great start.

Do you have a value proposition for your team that allows them to have something different than they would as part of your competitor's organization?

Peloton is a strong example here. Many Peloton instructors are influencers in society, using their voice to drive change. For example, Kendall Toole, a former Peloton instructor, spoke openly of her struggles with mental health and Peloton supported her mission of sharing this struggle. As a result, its members did not feel alone if they were fighting something similar.

Look back to the mission, vision, value statement from Chapter 10. Does it require any adjustments?

There may be no adjustment necessary, but these two sections pair nicely together. This is a good place to revisit prior thoughts and adjust them, if needed.

CHAPTER 20
EXIT STRATEGY

In sports, every athlete and team must think about the future, whether it's preparing for retirement, transitioning to coaching, or managing life after the final whistle blows. In business, an exit strategy serves a similar purpose: It's a plan for how you will leave or transition out of your business when the time comes. Having a clear, well-thought-out exit strategy is essential for ensuring a smooth transition, preserving the value of your business, and achieving your long-term financial and personal goals.

An exit strategy outlines the steps you will take to sell, transfer, or close your business. Whether you plan to sell to an outside buyer, pass the business on to family, or wind down operations, having a plan ensures that the process is as seamless and profitable as possible. In this chapter, we will explore the different types of exit strategies.

Why You Need an Exit Strategy: Ensuring a Smooth Transition

Just as athletes plan for life after their playing careers, business owners must plan for what will happen when they are ready to exit. An exit strategy allows you to control the narrative. Here are the key reasons to plan your exit:

- By planning your exit in advance, you can take steps to maximize the value of your business. This might include improving financial performance, strengthening customer relationships, or building a management team that can

run the business without you. A strong business is more attractive to potential buyers or successors.
- Without an exit plan, your business could face significant risks if you need to step away unexpectedly due to illness, retirement, or other unforeseen circumstances. An exit strategy helps mitigate these risks by ensuring that there is a clear plan in place for what will happen when you leave.
- Your exit strategy should align with your personal goals, whether that means achieving financial security, passing the business on to the next generation, or pursuing new ventures. Having a plan ensures that your exit aligns with your long-term vision.

Types of Exit Strategies: Finding the Right Fit for Your Business

There are several different types of exit strategies, each with its own advantages and challenges. The right exit strategy for your business will depend on your goals, the size and structure of your business, and your personal preferences. Here are some common exit strategies to consider:

SELLING THE BUSINESS

Selling your business to an outside buyer is one of the most common exit strategies. This could involve selling to another company (through a merger or acquisition), a private equity firm, or an individual buyer. The key to a successful sale is preparing your business to be as attractive as possible to potential buyers.

- Advantages: A sale can provide you with a significant financial return, giving you the capital to pursue other ventures or retire comfortably. Additionally, selling to an outside buyer allows you to fully exit the business and hand over control to someone else.

- Challenges: Finding the right buyer and negotiating a fair price can be challenging. The sale process can also take time and may involve legal, financial, and operational complexities.

PASSING THE BUSINESS TO FAMILY OR EMPLOYEES

Many business owners choose to keep the business in the family or transfer ownership to trusted employees through an employee stock ownership plan (ESOP) or management buyout. This strategy allows you to maintain a sense of continuity and ensure that the business remains in the hands of people you trust.

- Advantages: Transferring the business to family or employees can help preserve the legacy of the business and ensure that it continues to operate according to your vision. It can also provide a more gradual transition, allowing you to stay involved in the business during the handover period.
- Challenges: Family dynamics or employee management challenges can complicate the process. It's important to have clear agreements in place to avoid conflicts and ensure a smooth transition.

INITIAL PUBLIC OFFERING (IPO)

An IPO involves taking your business public by offering shares to the public for the first time. This strategy is often pursued by larger, more established businesses looking to raise capital and expand.

- Advantages: An IPO can provide significant financial rewards and raise the profile of your business. It also allows you to maintain some level of control if you choose to retain a portion of your shares.
- Challenges: Going public is a complex and expensive process that involves meeting regulatory requirements

and dealing with the scrutiny of shareholders and financial markets. It's typically only an option for larger businesses with a proven track record of success.

MERGING WITH ANOTHER COMPANY

Mergers involve combining your business with another company, often to create a larger, more competitive entity. This can be a way to exit while still ensuring that the business continues to grow and evolve.

- Advantages: Merging with another company can create synergies, increase market share, and provide financial rewards for both parties. It also allows for a more collaborative transition, as the new entity can benefit from both companies' strengths.
- Challenges: Mergers can be complex and may involve significant negotiation to ensure that both parties are satisfied with the terms. Additionally, there may be cultural or operational challenges as the two companies integrate.

CLOSING THE BUSINESS

In some cases, the best option may be to wind down operations and close the business. This might be the case if the business is no longer profitable, or if you are ready to retire and there are no viable buyers or successors.

- Advantages: Closing the business allows you to exit on your own terms and avoid the complexities of selling or transferring ownership. It also gives you the freedom to pursue other opportunities without the pressure of managing a business.
- Challenges: Closing a business can be emotionally difficult, especially if you have invested significant time and energy into building it. Additionally, there may be financial or legal obligations to address, such as settling debts or selling off assets.

Preparing for Your Exit: Key Steps to Take

Once you've chosen an exit strategy, it's important to start preparing for your exit well in advance. Here are the key steps to take:

IMPROVE FINANCIAL PERFORMANCE

Potential buyers or successors will be most interested in businesses with strong financials. Focus on improving your financial performance by increasing profitability, managing expenses, and streamlining operations. A healthy balance sheet and clear financial records will make your business more attractive to buyers.

BUILD A STRONG MANAGEMENT TEAM

If your business relies heavily on you for day-to-day operations, it may be difficult to sell or transfer ownership. Build a strong management team that can run the business independently, ensuring that it can thrive without your direct involvement.

GET YOUR LEGAL AND FINANCIAL AFFAIRS IN ORDER

Ensure that your legal and financial documents are up to date and in good order. This includes contracts, intellectual property rights, tax filings, and any outstanding liabilities. Having clear and organized records will make the transition smoother and reduce the risk of legal issues arising during the sale or transfer process.

VALUATE YOUR BUSINESS

Understanding the value of your business is essential for negotiating a fair sale or transfer. Work with a professional appraiser to assess the value of your business based on factors such as revenue, profit margins, market position, and assets. A clear understanding of your business's worth will help you make informed decisions during the exit process.

DEVELOP A TRANSITION PLAN

A successful exit involves more than just selling the business — it requires a smooth transition of ownership and operations. Develop a transition plan that outlines how you will hand over control, train successors, and manage customer relationships during the change. A well-executed transition ensures that the business continues to thrive after you leave.

Start With the End in Mind

When starting from scratch with a client and considering a new business, sometimes it helps to start with the end in mind. I like to use Google Maps and Apple Maps as a good analogy for this process. Since we have smart phones with maps, it has become common place to "just get in and drive" without any route planning. You can simply enter your destination and follow the blue dot as it adapts in real time — if you make a wrong turn or hit heavy traffic, it will re-route you. My professional experience allows me to be the blue dot for my clients. Utilizing my decades of experience, I help clients reach their end destination safely, rerouting them as needed along the way. I accompany them until they reach "the destination" — the exit.

Experienced coaches know the way, which is why teams hire them, trusting them to serve as the blue dot. Inter Miami brought David Beckham into the ownership group and shortly thereafter acquired Lionel Messi, arguably one of the best players the world has ever seen. Beckham's experience, both internationally and in the U.S., uniquely positioned him to attract Messi and other international stars to the organization. This led to almost instant success for Inter Miami: The first full year that Messi was involved, Inter Miami became the team to beat in MLS. It is a living example of experience and wisdom bringing success.

An experienced "blue dot" can be especially invaluable in emotionally charged decisions, like deciding how to exit a business. Planning an exit strategy is about more than just leaving your business. It's about ensuring that your hard work pays off and that your legacy continues. Whether you're selling, passing the business on to family, or winding down operations, a well-thought-out exit strategy allows you to leave on your own terms and secure your financial future.

By choosing the right exit strategy, preparing in advance, and managing the transition carefully, you can ensure that your business continues to succeed even after you've stepped away. Just as athletes plan for life after sports, business owners should plan for life after their business, ensuring that the next chapter is as rewarding as the last.

Questions for You to Answer, Plus a Podcast Example to Consider

Even if you're at the start of your business journey, it's worth considering these questions now:

- What do I think my exit might be?
- What timeline would I associate with this exit?
- What odds do I put on the likelihood of that happening?
- Have others exited their business like this? If so, who?

Now, let's look at how our fitness trainer turned podcaster might answer those queries.

What do you think your exit might be?

Our fitness trainer recognizes that most fitness businesses do not exist beyond the trainer. Although they have hopes to one day create something larger than herself, they are a realist and know that creating something larger is likely unattainable given the current budget. Thus, the podcast exit is simply an exit that is chosen. They will just stop producing the podcast if the purpose to develop content and create customers is no longer effective. However, it is possible that the podcast gets absorbed or acquired into a fitness or media platform if popular enough.

What timeline would you associate with this exit?

Assuming our trainer is in their late twenties, the podcast exit could be short- or long-lived. Since podcasting is a relatively new form of media, there is some uncertainty; however, radio, TV, and other media has existed for over one hundred years. We started with Over the Air. Over the Air turned into Cable. Cable turned to Satellite. Satellite turned to Streaming. Some version of this podcast can last a lifetime.

What odds do you put on the likelihood of that happening?

The odds of the trainer stopping are 100 percent. The odds of a sale or merger into another company are fairly small, maybe around 1 percent.

Have others exited their business like this? If so, who?

In 2021, Beachbody, an online streaming fitness company, entered a three-way merger with two other companies and became a publicly traded company, with an enterprise value of $2.9 billion.[8] It's extremely unlikely that our podcaster will achieve something similar. Being aware of the magnitude can put things in perspective. Fitness trainers exit the business every day, for reasons ranging from changing careers to aging out or losing their passion. Exiting is as simple as not doing it anymore, which makes this fairly easy to transition away from.

---

8 "The Beachbody Company, a Leader in Digital Fitness Streaming and Nutrition Solutions, to Become Publicly Traded Company," *Business Wire*, February 10, 2021, https://www.businesswire.com/news/home/20210210005414/en/The-Beachbody-Company-a-Leader-in-Digital-Fitness-Streaming-and-Nutrition-Solutions-to-Become-Publicly-Traded-Company.

PART III: FUNDAMENTALS OF BUSINESS SUCCESS

CHAPTER 21
OPTIMIZING AND ADAPTING FOR SUCCESS

In the world of business and sports, success is rarely accidental. Both business and soccer require strategy, discipline, adaptability, and leadership to achieve consistent results. The role of a business coach and a soccer coach is fundamentally the same: They guide, strategize, and push their teams to reach peak performance.

As a soccer player, you observe and act on the concepts you learn from various coaches to achieve better performance. Similarly, my young years were spent watching and learning from my parents in their roles as business owners, later going on to implement those learnings as a business owner myself.

It is a little easier to convey success as a soccer coach, because everyone is familiar in some way with the measurements of wins and losses. However, beyond wins and losses, coaches have another metric for success: developing players and having a positive lifelong impact on them. This is similar to how you might measure the success of a business coach, by a record of developing others and creating lasting impact. My clients recognize this, trusting that the wisdom and experience that has allowed for my own success can help them achieve theirs.

The fundamentals of that recipe for success are contained in this book. What is success? Is it all about the money? Is it more free time? There is not one answer here. Go back to the points you thought about or wrote down in Part I of this book. Those are "your" targets for success. Keep those in mind, as they will guide you through Part III of the book, where we build you a realistic way to start moving forward.

Realistic Structure for Getting Started

There are three fundamentals for starting any business:

1. Have something someone wants. This could be a product, service, or skill.
2. Find someone who values it. Identify potential initial clients or customers.
3. Enable an exchange. Establish a simple way to deliver your offering and receive payment.

Once these basics are met, we can build out external and internal structures in phases. I know this may seem like an elementary way to think about your business and it leaves a lot to be desired, but this is it! These are the fundamentals of any business.

External Structure

This phase establishes the visible, client-facing aspects of your business.

PRESENCE AND VISIBILITY

Name and brand basics: Choose a business name, basic logo, or tagline to represent your offering. Keep it simple but recognizable.

Online presence: Start with a basic website or social media profile where clients can find you, understand what you offer, and contact you.

Core marketing: Word-of-mouth communication and networking are powerful. Leverage personal networks or existing client relationships to gain initial traction.

SIMPLE LEGAL SETUP

Register the business: Choose a straightforward legal structure (like sole proprietorship or LLC) based on your needs.

Compliance basics: Get any essential permits, licenses, and business insurance. These basics vary by industry but provide a legal foundation.

BASIC FINANCIAL PROCESSES

Payment and invoicing: Set up a way to receive payments (e.g., a business bank account and basic invoicing software).

Tracking finances: Start simple. A spreadsheet for income and expenses will work, but basic accounting software can streamline things as you grow.

Internal Structure

These five elements form a cohesive internal framework, building a solid base to operate and grow your business effectively.

BUSINESS LEADERSHIP

Vision and direction: Define a clear purpose and long-term goals for the business. Regularly revisit this vision to ensure you're on track and motivated.

Decision making and strategy: Develop a habit of making informed decisions by setting time aside to analyze both current operations and future opportunities.

Leadership and culture: Even in a small business, setting a positive tone and values impacts everyone involved. Establish a culture of respect, learning, and accountability.

SALES AND MARKETING

Customer understanding: Gain insights into your customers' needs, preferences, and pain points. Regularly engage with them to keep these insights fresh.

Marketing strategy: Use targeted, cost-effective methods to reach your audience (e.g., social media, networking, and referrals). Start with simple messaging focused on your unique value.

Sales process: Develop a consistent approach to closing sales, including tracking leads, following up, and converting them into loyal customers. A simple CRM tool or even a spreadsheet can help keep track of this process.

OPERATIONS AND MANAGEMENT

Workflow documentation: Create standard procedures for key tasks. This helps ensure consistency and can later be used to onboard new team members.

Resource management: Keep track of your essential resources, such as equipment, inventory, or tools, to ensure you have what you need when you need it.

Customer service: Design a responsive, customer-centered approach to handle inquiries and feedback. This is key for building long-term relationships and positive reviews.

PRODUCT/SERVICE DEVELOPMENT

Continuous improvement: Regularly evaluate your offerings based on customer feedback and market changes. Small, incremental improvements can make a significant impact over time.

Quality control: Set clear standards for quality, ensuring your product or service consistently meets expectations. Quality builds trust and enhances your reputation.

Innovation: Stay open to new ideas, whether it's enhancing a current product or introducing a new service. Being adaptable in your offerings keeps you relevant and competitive.

FINANCIAL HEALTH AND SUSTAINABILITY

Budgeting and expense management: Track your income and expenses closely. Regularly review your budget to ensure you're allocating resources effectively.

Cash flow management: Ensure you have sufficient cash on hand to cover operational expenses and emergencies. A basic cash flow projection can help you anticipate needs.

Profit tracking and reinvestment: Monitor profitability and, as feasible, reinvest a portion back into the business to fuel growth in the other internal areas.

This framework provides a straightforward yet comprehensive internal structure, giving you stability while maintaining the flexibility to grow.

From the Essentials to the Formal Structure: A Growth Timeline

STAGE 1: 0–18 MONTHS | FOUNDATION PHASE

At this point the primary focus is essentials, external structure, and basic internal structure.

Essentials only: Start with the fundamentals — something people want, someone who values it, and a way to exchange value. Focus on delivering quality, securing customer satisfaction, and maintaining financial health.

Early external structure: Create visibility with a basic online presence, start networking, and leverage word-of-mouth communication to grow your client base.

Basic internal systems: Begin by tracking finances, customer interactions, and basic workflows. These can be simple (e.g., spreadsheets or basic accounting software).

Iteration 1: Revisit your offerings, customer base, and feedback. Adjust pricing, product features, or processes as you refine what's working best.

Milestones: Consistent revenue, a basic but effective customer service process, and a reliable way to deliver your offering.

STAGE 2: 18–36 MONTHS | EXPANSION PHASE

The primary focus at this stage is the internal structure expansion, and strategic sales and marketing.

Enhanced external structure: Invest in branding and an improved online presence (e.g., upgraded website, social media engagement, or content marketing).

Strengthen sales and marketing: Expand your customer acquisition strategies. Introduce a more structured sales process, consider using a CRM, and formalize lead generation efforts.

Internal structure development: Establish clearer workflows and documentation, refine financial tracking with formal accounting practices, and expand cash flow management. You might begin segmenting teams or tasks (even if you're the only one executing) to mimic future roles.

Iteration 2: Analyze performance data from the previous eighteen months, reviewing sales patterns, customer feedback, and financial health. Adjust strategies, streamline processes, and continue developing what's working.

Milestones: A stronger brand presence, consistent sales process, deeper customer relationships, and a more refined financial strategy.

STAGE 3: 3-10 YEARS | MATURITY PHASE

The primary focus is now full formal structure implementation and sustainable growth.

Formal structure: Begin implementing aspects of the full formal structure, including risk management, team building, and deeper financial forecasting. Develop a customer experience strategy and further define internal and external structures.

Advanced sales and marketing: Shift focus toward customer retention and loyalty programs. Strengthen your sales strategy by exploring new channels, partnerships, or distribution options.

Operational efficiency: Invest in technology and infrastructure to streamline operations (e.g., automation, inventory management software, or enhanced customer service platforms). Start building a management team or delegating key responsibilities.

Iteration 3: Conduct a comprehensive business review every few years. Adjust processes, evaluate customer satisfaction, and address areas needing improvement. This review ensures that all formal structure elements remain aligned with your business's evolving goals.

Milestones: A resilient business model, loyal customer base, optimized operations, and a full internal and external structure aligned with growth.

BEYOND 10 YEARS | LEGACY AND EVOLUTION PHASE

In this final phase, the primary focus is sustainable, scalable growth and an exit strategy.

Business sustainability: Focus on long-term sustainability through environmental, social, and governance (ESG) practices. These efforts reinforce brand reputation and customer loyalty.

Formalized exit strategy: Begin considering or formalizing an exit plan, whether it's succession, sale, or a transition to new leadership.

Iteration 4 and beyond: Periodically reevaluate all elements of your business (market research, risk management, customer experience) to stay competitive. Iterative improvement ensures resilience and keeps your business aligned with market changes.

Milestones: A sustainable business model, a fully developed team, industry reputation, and a clear plan for future transitions.

CHAPTER 22
THE POWER OF ITERATION

Think of this chapter like training for a soccer player. A soccer player evolves season to season, working on weaknesses, developing skills, and using past experience to make the next game better. You will do the same thing in your business. The concepts discussed here are things that you might address during periods of reflection, when something goes wrong, or during downtime.

The Power of Iteration: Building Resilience

In the journey from starting a business to establishing a lasting, successful enterprise, resilience is built through continuous iteration. This process involves regularly revisiting and refining each area of your business to adapt to new challenges, evolving customer needs, and industry shifts.

REFINING THE PRODUCT/SERVICE OFFERING

As your business matures, the product or service you started with may need updates or expansions to remain competitive. Iterative refinement ensures that your offering consistently meets or exceeds customer expectations.

Make it a regular practice to gather and apply customer feedback, using insights to enhance product features, improve quality, or even add new offerings. By staying tuned to your audience, you ensure that your product or service stays relevant and valued.

As your operations grow, establishing stronger quality standards helps maintain consistency. Iteration here involves implementing more efficient quality control processes to reduce errors and enhance customer satisfaction.

EXPANDING SALES AND MARKETING EFFORTS

Effective sales and marketing are dynamic, evolving processes. Iteration in these areas lets you test, refine, and scale your efforts, building upon initial successes to reach larger, more targeted audiences.

Over time, different marketing channels may become more or less effective. Regularly assess which channels deliver the highest return and focus resources accordingly. Experiment with new approaches—such as content marketing, social media, or customer referral programs—and adjust based on performance data.

Streamline and personalize your sales approach through tools like CRM software, which can track customer interactions and provide data for refining your sales tactics. Iteratively refining your sales process creates a more responsive and effective sales funnel that adapts to changing market conditions and customer behaviors.

STRENGTHENING OPERATIONS AND MANAGEMENT

In business, operational efficiency is foundational. Iterative improvements to operations allow you to optimize processes, reduce waste, and handle growth sustainably. Regularly evaluating your management practices helps align your team and systems with your evolving business needs.

Identify repetitive tasks and document them to create efficient workflows. This iterative approach to documentation simplifies onboarding, training, and delegation as your team expands.

Integrate new technologies as they become available, from automation tools to advanced data analytics. Periodic upgrades improve efficiency and reduce manual workloads, allowing your team to focus on strategic initiatives.

Developing Business Leadership and Culture

Leadership evolves with each stage of business. Iterative improvement in leadership and company culture fosters resilience, attracting talent, nurturing innovation, and adapting to change.

Regularly revisit your mission and values to ensure that your leadership approach stays aligned with your evolving goals. Leadership isn't static; it grows with your business, becoming more inclusive, strategic, and adaptive over time.

Foster a culture of learning and accountability. Encourage feedback and empower team members to suggest improvements. This approach strengthens your team's connection to the business's purpose, creating a resilient, cohesive culture that supports long-term success.

ENHANCING FINANCIAL HEALTH AND SUSTAINABILITY

Financial resilience is a critical part of long-term business health. Iteratively improving financial practices, from cash flow management to budgeting, builds a strong financial foundation capable of withstanding fluctuations and supporting growth.

As revenue patterns shift, periodically reassess your budget and allocate resources where they will have the most significant impact. This approach helps you maintain financial stability while pursuing growth opportunities.

Cash flow is the lifeblood of your business. Regularly analyze cash flow patterns and identify areas to improve liquidity, such as invoicing efficiencies, expense management, or negotiating with vendors. Iterative adjustments ensure financial sustainability, allowing you to handle both opportunities and challenges with confidence.

Iteration as a Continuous Process

Iteration is a sustained practice that keeps your business responsive, agile, and aligned with its core purpose and goals. Each iterative improvement strengthens the core of your business, creating a resilient structure that adapts over time. Through continuous refinement across your product, sales, operations, leadership, and financial health, your business becomes more adaptable, customer-focused, and robust.

CHAPTER 23
PUTTING IT INTO PRACTICE

Now let's put it into practice. Although the exercise is an example, it might help you see some different ways to think about your plan. Imagine you've started with a simple product in your garage. You don't have a factory, marketing team, or even a website yet — just an idea you're passionate about, some essential materials, and a vision. Growing from this stage to a thriving business can happen step by step, each phase building on the last. Here's how the realistic structure might look for someone moving their product from garage beginnings to a larger-scale operation.

Starting Point: The Essentials

In the garage, it's all about the basics. You just need:

- A product. You've created something valuable, unique, and useful.
- People who value it. Friends, family, and early adopters who recognize the potential of your product and are willing to pay for it.
- A way to sell it. Maybe you're accepting cash, running orders through a basic online marketplace, or even selling directly to local contacts.

This phase is about testing your product, making sure it's meeting needs, and ensuring it holds up in real-world use. Like any homegrown project, it's likely you're learning as you go —

refining the product, adapting based on feedback, and building confidence that it has staying power.

Building the External Structure: Moving Out of the Garage

As demand grows, it's time to take the next steps to establish a professional front for your business, moving out of the garage and creating a more public presence for your product. This requires:

- Branding and visibility. Create a name, logo, or tagline that represents your product. This is your "storefront" — even if it's online — to make your brand memorable and accessible.
- Online presence. Transition from word-of-mouth sales to a basic website or social media page. This gives customers a place to learn about your product, place orders, and share their experiences.
- Basic legal and financial setup. Register your business, secure any necessary permits, and set up a simple invoicing or payment system. This external structure gives your business legitimacy and ensures you can handle increasing customer inquiries smoothly.

Each of these steps brings your product one step closer to being a professional, reputable offering rather than just a garage project, setting the stage for bigger growth by getting the basics in place.

Building the Internal Structure: Creating Processes and Scaling Up

With interest growing, it's time to look at your internal operations and create repeatable processes to streamline production, manage finances, and handle customer interactions. Here's how the internal structure fits in as you scale up

BUSINESS LEADERSHIP (DEFINING GOALS AND VALUES)

Step into the role of business leader by shaping your vision, setting clear goals, and making strategic decisions. Define and document your company's core values, then communicate them to your team so they guide every decision and interaction. Establishing these values now will set the tone for future growth and a strong company culture.

SALES AND MARKETING (GENERATING DEMAND)

Start actively marketing your product through targeted outreach, whether through social media, partnerships, or direct advertising. Develop a basic sales process — how do customers learn about your product, try it out, and make a purchase? Creating this predictable path for customers turns one-time buyers into loyal customers.

OPERATIONS AND MANAGEMENT (STREAMLINING PRODUCTION)

Scaling up often means shifting from handmade or one-off production to a more streamlined approach. Document your process, source materials efficiently, and consider outsourcing some tasks if needed. This step helps you handle higher demand without compromising quality.

PRODUCT DEVELOPMENT (EVOLVING WITH FEEDBACK)

Every successful product evolves with feedback. As more customers use your product, gather insights and look for opportunities to improve. Even small adjustments — like refining packaging or upgrading materials — can elevate customer satisfaction and position your product for broader appeal.

FINANCIAL HEALTH AND SUSTAINABILITY (BUDGETING FOR GROWTH)

Managing finances as you grow requires planning for larger expenses, like marketing campaigns or bulk material purchases. Set a budget, monitor cash flow, and reinvest carefully to support further expansion. This step ensures you can sustain growth rather than burning out financially as demand increases.

Continuous Iteration: Revisit and Refine with Each New Milestone

As the business grows, it's essential to revisit each element periodically. Just as you refined the product in the early garage days, each new stage brings lessons and opportunities for improvement. Iteration ensures that you're responsive to market changes, customer feedback, and operational needs, adapting as you transition from a small operation to a sustainable business.

This iterative approach makes each stage stronger, building on the last and preventing small issues from turning into big problems. By continuously revisiting your product, processes, and structure, you're able to adapt, innovate, and grow beyond the original garage idea into a fully realized business, ready to serve a broad and loyal customer base.

PART IV: BEHAVE LIKE A BUSINESS OWNER (BLABO)

CHAPTER 24
BECOMING THE BUSINESS OWNER YOU WANT TO BE

Ernest Hemingway once said, "There is nothing noble in being superior to your fellow man; true nobility is being superior to your former self." This is the essence of entrepreneurship — not aiming to outdo others, but to grow beyond who you were yesterday. Many of the greatest business owners started without having all the answers or a perfect plan. They started with a commitment to become better, to take action, and to learn from each step.

Imagine this: A young entrepreneur has an idea — a solution to a problem they've encountered countless times. The idea sits in their mind for months, maybe even years. Every day, they dream of what it could become. But as time passes, they notice others bringing similar ideas to life. Instead of inspiring them, it stirs doubt. Why should I compete? What if I'm not ready?

Then, a mentor shares Hemingway's words: It's not about being the best, but about improving yourself day by day. That's when it clicks. The young entrepreneur decides to take a small step, then another, and then another. Each step builds confidence. Each challenge tackled feels like a triumph. And before long, they've grown their idea into something real. No longer comparing themselves to others but constantly refining their own path, measuring progress only by how far they've come.

To truly Behave Like a Business Owner, commit to action. The journey isn't just about setting up a business, or about finances or operations. It's about showing up for yourself, challenging yesterday's limits, and pushing toward the business you envision. Being an owner isn't a one-time decision; it's a series of choices to step up, learn, adjust, and grow.

Are you ready to take the steps? To create, execute, assess, and refine? That's how you become a business owner — not by waiting for perfect timing, but by acting and constantly working to become better than who you were yesterday.

To guide you in Behaving Like a Business Owner (BLABO), we'll reference the workbook from Part III and align each action step with specific items you've already outlined. By grouping the workbook sections under these actions, you can see how your answers build the foundation you need to take ownership and grow confidently. You can start to look at the details, tree by tree.

1. Create Your Business / Entity

WORKBOOK SECTIONS:

- Business plan: Define your mission, goals, and unique value.
- Legal structure and compliance: Choose a business structure and meet any legal requirements.

Creating your business entity is the first official step. With your mission, target market, and goals defined in your business plan, you have clarity on why you're starting. By choosing the appropriate legal structure and ensuring compliance, you formalize your business, giving it a solid legal foundation. This step is about claiming your space as a business owner and stepping into that role with purpose.

2. Establish Your Finances

WORKBOOK SECTIONS:

- Funding and financial management: Identify your funding sources, create a basic budget, and track finances.
- Financial health and sustainability: Plan for cash flow, budgeting, and profit goals.

To succeed, your business must be financially secure. Your financial planning in the workbook gives you the blueprint to manage resources, understand your expenses, and set realistic income goals. Establishing solid financial practices from the start helps you maintain control over growth, handle unexpected challenges, and make your vision sustainable.

3. Establish Your Operations

WORKBOOK SECTIONS:

- Operations and management: Outline workflows, manage resources, and set customer service standards.
- Technology and infrastructure: Identify tools and technology to streamline processes.

Operations are the backbone of your business. Your workbook answers on workflows, resource management, and customer service give you an operational plan that keeps everything moving efficiently. By setting up basic systems and selecting essential tools, you make it possible to scale and adapt without losing quality. This phase is about creating a reliable, consistent framework that customers can trust.

4. Communicate "I'm Open for Business"

WORKBOOK SECTIONS:

- Branding and marketing: Develop your brand identity and choose key marketing channels.
- Sales strategy: Define your target audience, pricing strategy, and sales approach.

Once your operations are ready, it's time to tell the world you're open. Your brand, messaging, and sales approach will be how customers first perceive you. With clear branding, an approachable sales process, and chosen channels to reach your audience, you signal confidence and professionalism, setting the stage for a lasting first impression.

5. Execute on the Operations

WORKBOOK SECTIONS:

- Product or service development: Outline your offering, quality standards, and plans for improvement.
- Sales and marketing: Execute your marketing strategy and reach out to customers.

Executing operations means putting everything into action — from delivering products and services to engaging with customers. Each sale, customer interaction, and product delivered shapes your brand's reputation. By following your workbook's strategies on product quality and customer service, you can ensure consistent, positive experiences that build trust and loyalty.

6. Perform Operational Assessments/Adjustments

WORKBOOK SECTIONS:

- Operations and management: Review workflows and streamline where needed.
- Technology and infrastructure: Update tools and systems as needed to improve efficiency.

As your business grows, operations will need regular assessment. Identify what's working and what could be improved based on customer feedback and evolving needs. If processes feel slow or outdated, it might be time to adjust. This step ensures that your business stays agile and efficient, ready to handle increased demands without missing a beat.

7. Get Customer Feedback

WORKBOOK SECTIONS:

- Customer experience: Define the ideal customer journey and gather feedback.
- Networking and partnerships: Build relationships and encourage referrals.

Customer feedback is essential for growth. With a simple system in place for collecting feedback, you'll know how well you're meeting customer needs. By understanding the customer journey and maintaining a strong network, you position your business to evolve with the market and build loyalty.

8. Perform Financial Assessments/Adjustments

WORKBOOK SECTIONS:

- Financial health and sustainability: Revisit budgeting, cash flow, and profit goals.
- Funding and financial management: Adjust based on business growth and financial performance.

Financial assessment keeps you on track for growth. Regularly reviewing your budget and cash flow, as outlined in your workbook, lets you adjust for any changes like increased expenses or new revenue streams. Financial adjustments allow you to reinvest in what's working and stay financially healthy.

9. Execute Change and Growth Management

WORKBOOK SECTIONS:

- Adaptability and innovation: Keep your business flexible, update products, and encourage new ideas.
- Exit strategy: Define your long-term vision and prepare for transitions.

Growth is exciting but requires adaptability. Your workbook guidance on staying innovative and planning for the future equips you to manage changes smoothly. Whether expanding product lines, adjusting for market trends, or planning for an exit, this step ensures that your business can evolve and thrive without losing its foundation.

Ready to Dive Deeper?

Each of these steps, when combined with your workbook responses, guides you in building a well-rounded business. This isn't just about creating a company — it's about embodying the role of a business owner, taking decisive actions, and continuously working to refine and improve your business. Ready to dive deeper? Being a business owner takes a lot of work, and nobody can do it alone. At some point, you'll need to expand your team and consult outside expertise. When you're ready to take the next step in your business, reach out to me. I would love to be part of your team and see how I can guide you in the next phase of your business.

CHAPTER 25
BLABO CHECKLIST

Yes, another checklist! Many of these concepts repeat what was previously discussed. However, just like an athlete, you have to keep "training" and fine tuning your business. This checklist is designed to help you during your operational phase of business. You will refine your business frequently, and this accountability tool can help.

This checklist gives you a high-level view of the core actions that embody BLABO, ensuring that you're always moving forward with purpose and structure. Use this as a reference to stay on track, measure your progress, and confidently take action in growing your business.

☑ **CREATE YOUR BUSINESS/ENTITY**

<u>Define mission and goals:</u> Outline your mission, goals, and unique value for a clear foundation.

<u>Choose legal structure:</u> Select the appropriate legal structure (LLC, sole proprietorship, etc.) and ensure compliance with necessary legal requirements.

☑ **ESTABLISH YOUR FINANCES**

<u>Set up budget and funding:</u> Identify funding sources, create a basic budget, and track expenses.

<u>Plan financially for growth:</u> Ensure cash flow, profit margins, and sustainability by assessing financial health regularly.

☑ ESTABLISH YOUR OPERATIONS

<u>Define workflows:</u> Set up consistent processes for delivering products or services efficiently.

<u>Implement technology and infrastructure:</u> Choose essential tools to streamline operations and improve efficiency.

☑ COMMUNICATE "I'M OPEN FOR BUSINESS"

<u>Branding and marketing:</u> Develop your brand identity and select key marketing channels.

<u>Engage in sales strategy:</u> Define your target audience, pricing, and customer acquisition strategy.

☑ EXECUTE ON THE OPERATIONS

<u>Deliver consistently:</u> Follow workflows and quality standards to maintain a reliable customer experience.

<u>Leverage resources:</u> Manage inventory, technology, and staffing effectively to meet customer demand.

☑ PERFORM OPERATIONAL ASSESSMENTS AND ADJUSTMENTS

<u>Review efficiency and customer feedback:</u> Regularly assess workflows, resource use, and customer input.

<u>Update technology and processes:</u> Adjust systems as needed to improve productivity and quality.

☑ GET CUSTOMER FEEDBACK

<u>Collect feedback:</u> Use surveys, follow-ups, and social media to gather customer insights.

<u>Make improvements based on feedback:</u> Address any recurring issues and adjust offerings or service as needed.

☑ PERFORM FINANCIAL ASSESSMENTS AND ADJUSTMENTS

<u>Review financial metrics:</u> Regularly evaluate cash flow, expenses, and profit margins.

<u>Adjust budget and pricing:</u> Update budget allocations and pricing to meet business goals.

☑ EXECUTE CHANGE AND GROWTH MANAGEMENT

<u>Identify growth opportunities:</u> Stay alert to market trends and customer demand to inform growth.

<u>Manage resources for scale:</u> Allocate resources wisely to expand without sacrificing quality.

PART V: THE EXIT

CHAPTER 26
EVERYONE WILL EXIT THEIR BUSINESS

There is one universal truth in business ownership: At some point, everyone will leave their business. Whether it's through a carefully planned transition, an unexpected sale, or unforeseen circumstances, every business owner will face this reality. The question is not if you will exit your business but how and when. Recognizing this inevitability is not a matter of pessimism; it's a matter of preparation and control.

For many entrepreneurs, the thought of exiting their business is something they push far into the future, or worse, avoid entirely. Perhaps your focus is on daily operations, managing growth, or tackling the next challenge, and thinking about leaving feels distant or irrelevant. However, by not considering your exit, you risk relinquishing control over what could be one of the most significant events of your life.

The truth is, your exit will likely be the culmination of your efforts, the moment when your business either rewards you for your hard work or leaves you grappling with regrets. The difference lies in whether you approach your exit intentionally or leave it to chance.

Envisioning the Future: The Key to Intentional Exit

Having a vision for your business's future is not just about setting goals for the next quarter or year; it's about considering the entire lifecycle of your enterprise, including its eventual conclusion.

Knowing where you want to end up helps you make better decisions in the present. If you plan to sell your business, you may focus on building value and establishing systems that appeal to potential buyers. If you aim to pass it down to family, you might prioritize stability and succession planning.

A thoughtful approach to your business's future can also help you prepare for the unexpected and protect what you've built. Unexpected events like health issues, economic downturns, or changes in personal circumstances can force an unplanned exit.

Finally, planning ahead gives you time to grow your business strategically, making it more attractive to buyers, partners, or successors. An intentional exit ensures you extract the maximum value from your hard work.

Intention vs. Reaction: Taking Control of Your Legacy

When it comes to exiting your business, there are two paths: intentional exits and reactive exits.

Intentional exits happen on your terms. They might involve selling your business to a strategic buyer, passing it on to a family member or key employee, or winding it down gracefully. Intentional exits allow you to:

- Set the timeline that works best for you.
- Plan for tax-efficient transitions.
- Preserve your business's legacy and protect employees or stakeholders.

Reactive exits occur when you're forced to leave due to unforeseen circumstances like illness, burnout, financial trouble, or sudden offers. Reactive exits often lead to:

- Reduced bargaining power or sale price.
- Emotional and financial strain.
- A loss of control over how your business operates post exit.

By thinking about your future exit now, you can avoid being at the mercy of external events. Even if your timeline is decades away, having a plan — or at least a direction — puts you in control of your business's ultimate destiny.

Starting with the Future in Mind

To begin planning for your eventual exit, start by asking yourself:

- What do I want my business to look like when I leave? Is it thriving under new ownership, a family legacy, or sold to fund my next adventure?
- What do I want to achieve from my exit? Financial security, freedom, or the satisfaction of knowing my employees and clients are cared for?
- How do I want to be remembered? As someone who built something impactful, as a mentor to others, or simply as a successful entrepreneur who knew when to step away?

These questions are not meant to overwhelm but to inspire reflection. By starting to envision your future now, you can align your efforts today with the legacy you wish to leave tomorrow.

Exit Options: Benchmarks for Aligning Today with Tomorrow

While a comprehensive exit strategy requires significant planning and expertise — enough to fill an entirely different book — this chapter is meant to provide a foundational understanding of various exit options. These ideas can help you align your present decisions with future possibilities. Common exit options are outlined below.

SALE TO A THIRD PARTY

Selling to an external buyer is one of the most common exit strategies for business owners. This approach typically involves marketing your business to potential buyers, negotiating a sale price, and transitioning ownership.

- Advantages: Provides an opportunity to maximize the financial value of the business, especially if sold during a strong market or period of growth.
- Challenges: Requires careful preparation to make the business attractive to buyers, including financial transparency and operational independence.

MERGERS AND ACQUISITIONS

In a merger or acquisition, your business combines with or is purchased by another company. This is often seen in industries where consolidation creates strategic advantages.

- Advantages: Can lead to a higher valuation by leveraging synergies between the two companies.
- Challenges: May involve cultural and operational integration, which can disrupt existing teams or processes.

EMPLOYEE/MANAGEMENT/TEAM BUYOUT

Selling the business to your employees or management team allows you to pass the reins to those who know the business intimately and have a vested interest in its success.

- Advantages: Preserves the business culture and legacy while rewarding loyal team members.
- Challenges: May require financing structures, such as loans or deferred payments, to make the purchase feasible for employees.

INITIAL PUBLIC OFFERING (IPO)

Taking a company public involves selling shares to the public through an IPO. This option is often reserved for businesses with significant growth potential and scalability.

- Advantages: Provides substantial capital and liquidity while increasing the company's visibility and credibility.
- Challenges: Involves extensive regulatory compliance, costs, and the need to meet shareholder expectations.

FAMILY SUCCESSION PLANNING

Passing your business to family members is a common choice for those who want to preserve the legacy within the family. This requires grooming successors and preparing them for leadership roles.

- Advantages: Maintains family ownership and can preserve the founder's vision.
- Challenges: Requires careful planning to address family dynamics, skill gaps, and tax implications.

LIQUIDATION AND SALE

Liquidating assets and selling the business piecemeal is often a last resort but can be appropriate for businesses with valuable individual components.

- Advantages: Provides a straightforward way to exit if the business itself is not marketable as a whole.
- Challenges: Typically results in lower financial returns compared to other strategies.

REORGANIZATION/STRATEGIC PARTNERSHIP/RECAPITALIZATION

Restructuring the business, forming a strategic partnership, or recapitalizing (e.g., exchanging debt for equity) can serve as an alternative exit or transition plan.

- Advantages: Offers flexibility and can provide liquidity without completely exiting the business.
- Challenges: May involve complex financial and legal arrangements.

FRANCHISE MODELS

If your business has a replicable model, franchising can be a lucrative way to scale and eventually transition ownership of individual locations.

- Advantages: Generates passive income and allows for gradual disengagement from daily operations.
- Challenges: Requires significant upfront investment to establish a franchise system and attract franchisees.

BUY-SELL AGREEMENTS/PARTNER BUYOUT

Buy-sell agreements allow partners to establish clear terms for buying out an owner's share in the event of retirement, disability, or other triggering events.

- Advantages: Provides clarity and avoids disputes among partners.
- Challenges: Requires periodic updates to reflect changes in the business's value and circumstances.

Key Considerations When Choosing an Exit Plan

There are a few things to consider when deciding which exit plan is best for you.

BUSINESS VALUATION

Start by understanding the true value of your business. This provides a foundation for setting realistic expectations and negotiating effectively. Regular valuations can help you track your business's growth and prepare for market shifts.

TIMING

Timing is critical in maximizing the value of your exit. Consider market conditions, the business's performance, and personal readiness to step away. Exiting during a downturn can result in a lower valuation, whereas strong performance can significantly increase your leverage.

TAX IMPLICATIONS

Different exit strategies have varying tax consequences. A sale may trigger capital gains taxes, while transferring ownership to family members may involve gift or estate taxes. Consulting with tax professionals can help minimize liabilities.

LEGAL CONSIDERATIONS

Ensure compliance with all legal and regulatory requirements during the exit process. This might include updating contracts, ensuring intellectual property protections, and addressing employee agreements.

PERSONAL GOALS

Align your exit strategy with your long-term aspirations. Whether it's securing financial freedom, ensuring the continuity of your business, or stepping away gracefully, your personal goals should guide your decisions.

Structuring Your Exit for Certainty

Even in the case of an unplanned event — such as death, disability, or an unexpected market downturn — you can have structures in place to facilitate any of the exit goals above. Consider establishing:

- A succession plan to identify and prepare future leaders.
- A buy-sell agreement with partners or stakeholders.
- Emergency reserves or insurance policies to protect your family and the business in your absence.

By addressing these elements now, you create a safety net that ensures your business can continue to thrive — or transition smoothly — regardless of the circumstances. The question is: Do you have these structures in place? If not, what steps will you take today to prepare for tomorrow?

CONCLUSION
THE FINAL WHISTLE: DID YOU PLAY TO WIN?

You started this journey with the same 168 hours a week you'll finish with, just like every player, every coach, and every entrepreneur. Over the last twenty-nine chapters, you've explored the playbook of business best practices: strategy, structure, execution, resilience, and leadership. But a playbook alone doesn't win games or start a business. It's what you do with it that matters. Now that you've studied the field and learned the moves, the question shifts from what to do to what you'll actually do next. How will you spend the next 168 hours?

Business, like soccer, doesn't reward the one who knows the most drills. It rewards the one who consistently shows up, puts in the work, and adapts in real time. You may not have all the answers yet, and you don't need to. What you need is a bias toward thoughtful action — a willingness to make decisions, learn from them, and keep improving. Great businesses are not built in one perfect season. They're built over time through training, failing, reworking the strategy, and pushing forward.

As you walk off this page and back into your weekly 168, remember that clarity doesn't come all at once. It builds as you act. You may start solo, juggling multiple roles, wearing every jersey. But the goal is not to stay there. The goal is to build something bigger than yourself. You may build a team, a system, or a vision that runs even when you're not the one sprinting up the sidelines. Your commitment to improving, to leading, and to aligning your time with your purpose is what separates the hobbyist from the true business owner.

You've seen the tools, explored the tactics, and hopefully gained a clearer vision of what it means to build something that lasts. But don't confuse the final chapter with the final word. The next version of your business won't come from re-reading this book. It'll come from stepping onto the field and playing with what you've learned. That's where the real growth happens.

The whistle blows, and the next match begins. Whether you're just kicking off or already deep into your season, the fundamentals remain the same: Know your goals, use your time intentionally, build your team, and adjust as you go. You have the playbook, and the field is yours. Go build your picture, one decision, one hour, one day at a time!

YOUR JOURNEY, OUR EXPERTISE

As you've worked through this book, you've explored tools, strategies, and examples designed to help you build and grow a successful business. Along the way, you've considered how to structure your vision, navigate challenges, and align today's decisions with tomorrow's goals. These principles form the foundation of every thriving business, but even the best foundation needs support.

Those that commit to the work, weave it into their routines, and focus on the evolution of their business are poised to succeed. Just like athletes, some will win and some will lose. Doing what you can to enable your success, adapting when things are not going as planned, and remaining committed to the business is essential. Many start out with a clear path but get lost and need some direction. Sometimes it is the opposite: They need help getting started, but once started the picture is clear. When you face obstacles, do not hesitate to ask for help from strategic partners along the way.

At Papin CPA PLLC and Papin Law, PLLC, we are here to provide that support. Whether you're starting your first business, managing growth, or planning your exit, we bring a unique combination of accounting and legal expertise to guide you through every stage of your journey. Our goal is simple: to empower business owners like you to make informed, confident decisions that lead to lasting success. We do this by building long-term relationships to help clients thrive.

Maybe you're the kind of person who loves to roll up your sleeves and dive in yourself. You're passionate, resourceful, and determined to make things happen. If that's you, we encourage you to get out there and do it. Build, refine, and pursue your vision with the drive and energy that brought you to this book in the first place. The tools and strategies you've learned here are a great starting point, and there's no substitute for taking action.

For those moments when you hit a roadblock or find yourself needing expert guidance, know that we're here to help. What sets us apart isn't just our technical knowledge. It's our commitment to understanding your unique goals and crafting solutions tailored to your needs. We believe in partnering with you, not just as advisors but as advocates for your success. Whether it's navigating complex tax laws, structuring your business for growth, or planning for a smooth transition, we are ready to help you move forward with clarity and confidence. And where we are unable to do that, we have many strategic partners at our side ready to step in.

Whether you're ready to collaborate with a team that has your back or eager to chart your own course, the most important thing is to keep moving forward. Success belongs to those who take the leap, learn from their experiences, and keep striving.

The future of your business is yours to shape. So, go ahead, take that next step, and when you're ready, let's shape it together.

ABOUT THE AUTHOR

Christopher C. Papin challenges the way business owners get advised — and his credentials back it up. With over 20 years of professional experience serving small business owners, he brings multiple disciplinary perspectives as an attorney (Oklahoma, Texas, Colorado), CPA, and insurance producer. Licensed as a CPA in 2007 and attorney in 2008, his background spans work at a Fortune 500 company and years in tax and accounting serving small business owners at another local firm.

Based in Edmond, Oklahoma, Papin now serves clients nationally through an integrated advisory model that refuses the traditional silos: "Ask your lawyer. Check with your CPA. Call your insurance person." His experience serving small business owners taught him that separation creates blind spots. Today, through Papin CPA, Papin Law, and Papin Insurance, every client decision benefits from simultaneous legal, tax, and financial perspective — whether you're meeting in person or working remotely.

This integrated approach defines his specialization: business formation, succession planning, estate protection, tax optimization, and proactive strategic advisory. His philosophy is grounded in reality: "Too many business owners are focused on today's fires while missing tomorrow's opportunities. Our firm helps them stop reacting and start planning with clarity, strategy, and the right support in one place."

Papin hosts the BLABO podcast (Behave Like a Business Owner) and speaks nationally on business strategy, leadership, and change management psychology. Recent recognition includes *Forbes* Best-in-State CPA (2025), Thomson Reuters Advisory Accelerator Award (2024), Best in Class Accounting Firms - Workplace Diversity award (2024), Martindale-Hubbell AV Preeminent rating, Oklahoma Bar Foundation Fellow, and OKC BIZ Forty Under 40.

A Licensed USSF soccer coach and has served in various roles including Chairman of the board for Epworth Villa and Epworth Living, Inc., Papin applies his coaching philosophy to business: stop managing crises, start building clarity. Mission: distill complex business and tax strategy into actionable insights for entrepreneurs ready to think differently.

LET'S WORK TOGETHER

The ideas in this book come from nearly two decades of working with business owners at critical decision points. The philosophy — integrated perspective, proactive strategy, clarity over compliance — isn't theoretical. It's tested. It works.

If those ideas resonate with where your business is headed, Chris is available for consulting and speaking engagements.

SPEAKING ENGAGEMENTS:
Chris speaks on business strategy, leadership, change management, and the practical psychology of building successful teams. His signature talks blend business acumen with authentic coaching perspective. From boardrooms to conferences, his message resonates across industries.

GET IN TOUCH:
To inquire about speaking engagements or consulting opportunities, visit papinspeaks.com or email chris@papinspeaks.com.

PROFESSIONAL SERVICES:
For integrated strategy — combining tax planning, legal structure, business formation, succession planning, and ongoing advisory support — Chris brings the rare combination of attorney, CPA, and business coach expertise. He works with small business owners who understand that the best decisions come from seeing the full picture.

Papin CPA, PLLC: www.papincpa.com | (405) 531-9119

Papin Law, PLLC: www.papinlaw.com | (405) 531-9096

Chris also hosts the BLABO podcast (Behave Like a Business Owner), where he explores the real challenges small business owners face and the integrated perspective that changes outcomes. Search for BLABO on Apple Podcasts, Spotify, or wherever you get your podcasts.

www.ingramcontent.com/pod-product-compliance
Lightning Source LLC
LaVergne TN
LVHW021339080526
838202LV00004B/235